Néstor Ponce de León

The Columbus Gallery

Néstor Ponce de León

The Columbus Gallery

ISBN/EAN: 9783744677509

Printed in Europe, USA, Canada, Australia, Japan

Cover: Foto ©Thomas Meinert / pixelio.de

More available books at **www.hansebooks.com**

THE
COLUMBUS GALLERY.

THE

"DISCOVERER OF THE NEW WORLD"

AS REPRESENTED IN PORTRAITS, MONUMENTS, STATUES,
MEDALS AND PAINTINGS.

HISTORICAL DESCRIPTION

BY

NÉSTOR PONCE DE LEÓN

(ILLUSTRATED.)

N. PONCE DE LEÓN, PUBLISHER,
40 Broadway, New York
1893

INTRODUCTION.

Having, for a period of some years, investigated the subject of the portraits of Columbus, and embodied the results of my inquiries in an address recently delivered before the American Geographical Society, I feel myself better able than many others would be to form an opinion of the value and extent of Mr. Ponce de Leon's labors in this difficult field of inquiry. I have read in manuscript a large part of his work—I think nearly the whole of it, or, at least, sufficiently to ascertain the facts that he has brought together and the conclusions he has based upon them. As respects the facts, his labor has been most exhaustive. He has, in my opinion, ascertained everything that is now within the reach of the most diligent scholar. He is an accomplished linguist and has had the advantage of being able to read the works consulted in the language in which they were written, and has not been compelled, as many investigators are, to depend upon translations. This is of value, for I have found in my own investigation of this subject passages not only translated imperfectly, but, in some cases, so erroneously, as to be misleading. As to his conclusions, I found to my surprise—and I suppose it has been equally so to him—that although our investigations were conducted and our respective productions prepared entirely independent of each other, that we have arrived generally at the same results; so much so, in fact, as to give the appearance, in different parts, as if the one had been written from the other. During my acquaintance with him of some years, and as fellows of the Geographical Society, we have frequently conversed upon the subject of the portraits of Columbus, and in preparing my address I asked him—as he was especially competent to do so—to give me his opinion of the character of Columbus that I might give it in the address, in connection with that of others, upon this much contested question. In our mode of investigation, however, and in what we have respectively written, we have, as I have said, worked independently, and it was not until our labors were completed and what we had written was ready for publication, that I found how much we agreed in the results arrived at.

I make this statement, as my own production is prior in point of time, having been delivered as my annual address before a society of which I am the President, and it is now printed in the Journal of that society. I felt that it was due to Mr. Ponce de León that no reader of his book should get an impression that he was in any way indebted to my prior publication, and that he should receive, as he is entitled to, the full benefit of the extensive researches he has made and the conclusions he has founded upon them.

In giving him the high praise which is due to him for his labors, I regret that he did not include in this book what he says in his preface he contemplated in respect to the general subject of Columbus. He is the best informed gentleman with whom I have conversed upon everything relating to the great discoverer, and whatever he may give to the public upon that subject will be reliable and valuable.

CHAS. P. DALY.

March 29. 1893.

PREFACE

It was my original intention, when I undertook the publication of this book, to have it embrace not only a complete Columbian Iconography, but also a series of essays bearing upon the most important events in the life of the Discoverer of our Continent. That portion of the book, however, relating to the portraits, monuments, statues and paintings, has become so extensive that I have been compelled to leave for a subsequent work the treatment of those interesting particulars which embrace studies concerning the place where Columbus was born: the date of his birth; the facts known or supposed to be known about his life before he entered the service of the Catholic Kings; the persons who protected him, and their participation in the enterprise; the source from whence were derived the funds employed in the first expedition; his relations with the brothers Pinzon; the place of his first landfall; his administration of the lands discovered or colonized by him; the causes of his imprisonment; the place and date of his death; the resting-place of his remains; his character; and, finally, many other points of less importance about his life which have been hidden under a thick veil until our time, when some historians and critics, after many efforts, have been able to partially raise it, and throw true light on some of those much controverted questions. My object was to present in this work all their discoveries, but I found this field to be so wide that it is even more extensive than the book I now offer to the reader.

As I have written this book in a language which is not my native tongue, and as I am fully aware that my knowledge of all its intricacies is rather deficient, I have called to my aid the services of a former officer of the British Army, who, besides being a graduate of the Oxford University, is a professional journalist, and has occupied important positions here on some of the best reviews and magazines,—Mr. A. C. Stevens, who has revised all my copy and corrected its numerous errors. With great pleasure I take advantage of this opportunity to tender him my best thanks for his most useful services.

I also wish to acknowledge the kindness of many other persons to whom I am equally indebted for pictures, descriptions and notes referring to the subject. Among them I must especially mention Ex-Chief Justice Charles P. Daly, President of the American Geographical Society: Mr. William E. Curtis; the Editor of the Cosmopolitan Magazine; Mr. George C. Hurlburt, Librarian of the American Geographical Society; Mr. Wilberforce Eames, of the Lenox Library; Mrs. Helen C. Conant; and Messrs. Ernesto de Zaldo, Benjamín Giberga, Arturo Cuyás, Juan Romeu, and N. Hammelberg, of this city; Mr. Charles F. Gunther, of Chicago; Messrs. Carlos I. Párraga, José M. Ramírez Arellano, José S. Jorrín, and Héctor de Saavedra, of Havana, and finally Mr. Nicolás Domínguez Cowan, of the City of Mexico.

NESTOR PONCE DE LEÓN.

NEW YORK, APRIL 1, 1893.

THE COLUMBUS GALLERY.

FOUR centuries have scarcely elapsed since Columbus set his foot for the first time on American soil, yet dense darkness already covers almost every one of the most important acts of his life. Although it may be considered as positive that he was born at Genoa, there is not a single trustworthy document in existence which proves it in an incontrovertible manner, and over twenty different places contend for the honor of having been his birthplace.

The date of his birth is also unknown, and is a point on which there is a great diversity of opinion among historians: some fix it in 1430, others twenty-six years later, in 1456, and each one of them alleges in defence of his opinion reasons which to all appearances are well-founded.

Nobody can explain in a satisfactory manner his career during the long period preceding his entering the service of the Catholic Kings. The source of the funds employed in fitting out the petty squadron with which he achieved his great discovery has given rise to a multitude of absurd fables and stories, the most important of which is that which refers to the pawning of the jewels and ornaments of Isabella the Catholic, a tradition the falsity of which has been shown in the most positive manner by Mr. Cesareo Fernandez Duro, one of the most competent authorities on this point, a great admirer of the famous Queen, and than whom no greater champion of the glories of Spain can be found.

The type and size of the vessels with which the great undertaking was accomplished is also a matter of doubt. It is likewise disputed and, in my opinion, it will never be positively known, which was the spot of the first landfall. The exact date of his death is still uncertain, the house in which he died is unknown, and even the resting place of his remains is a matter of contention! Such was the indifference of his contemporaries to the glory of the man who accomplished the most wonderful discovery ever dreamed of by the human mind, the man who rent the veil which shrouded the Sea of Darkness and revealed to an astonished Old World a New World hitherto unknown!

How could we expect that ungrateful generation to have taken the trouble to preserve for posterity, either on board or canvas, in marble or bronze, the lineaments of the unlucky navigator, who, forsaken by those whom he had benefited and enriched, died at a miserable inn in Valladolid, when none of the contemporary writers, not even his personal friend, the historian and first Chronicler of the Indies, Peter Martyr, deigned to mention in his works the date of the death of the illustrious Admiral?

The grand figure of Columbus, his genius, his unhappy life, the ingratitude with which he was treated by those whom he had made powerful and rich, have ever awakened in me the greatest interest and the deepest sympathy. In the course of my studies on the history of my country, I have had occasion to investigate many of the obscure or dubious facts relative to the life of the Admiral, and although I am not a hero-worshipper, nor do I consider Columbus an indispensable factor in the history of humanity, yet I admire him as one of the greatest men who ever existed, and who, if not the hero, the martyr or the apostle depicted by the mystic Roselly de Lorgues, is very far from being the pirate, thief, coward and forger, represented by his unjust detractor, the distinguished American writer, Aaron Goodrich. In truth, judging Columbus with strict justice and according to the moral canons of his times, he is entitled to be considered as one of the best and purest men of that period of ferocity and demoralization.

One of the many points which I have carefully investigated has been the personal appearance of the Admiral. In vain have I tried to find some portrait or monument representing him more or less trustworthily. I have in my collection very nearly five hundred so-called portraits of Columbus, many of which are taken from statues, etc., and I have examined, perhaps, double this number. They differ so widely that they cannot, under any circumstances, represent the same man.

After a very careful examination, I have found that they can be reduced to about thirty-five or forty types, of which the others are copies with greater or lesser changes.

The pictures and statues of Columbus may be divided into three great groups, to wit:

First. Pictures and engravings that were, perhaps, taken from life at different periods of his career, and copies of them which are more or less variations from the originals.

Second. Pictures, engravings, statues and bas-reliefs executed by their authors in strict accordance with the descriptions of the Admiral which his contemporaries have left.

Third. Imaginary pictures, engravings and statues by various artists or so-called artists.

I will, hereinafter, present copies and descriptions of the most important among them; but I believe it would be well to transcribe now the descriptions of the Admiral left by Peter Martyr, Oviedo, Las Casas, and Ferdinand Columbus, or whoever it was that compiled the *Historie* published under his name.

Peter Martyr describes him "as a man of tall stature, ruddy color, well-built and of good appearance."

Oviedo (*Book II. Chap II.*) says he was "a man of good stature and aspect, tall, rather than medium-sized, of vigorous build, with brilliant eyes, and well proportioned as to the rest of his face; very red hair and with a face somewhat ruddy and freckled; gracious when he wanted to be so, full of ire when his passions were roused."

Las Casas (*Historia de las Indias, Book I. Chap. II.*) says: "As to his exterior person and corporal proportions, he was tall rather than medium-sized; the face long and commanding; aquiline nose, light eyes, complexion fair, tending to a deep red. The beard and hair when he was a young man were fair, but very soon turned white on account of his many toils; finally, in his person and venerable aspect, he presented the appearance of a person of high position and authority and worthy of all reverence."

Ferdinand Columbus, his son, in (*Chap. III.*) of the book attributed to him, says: "The Admiral was a man of good appearance, above the medium height, with long face and somewhat prominent cheek-bones, and of average weight. He had an aquiline nose, light eyes, fair complexion and very ruddy. When a youth his hair was fair, but at thirty years of age it had all turned white."

I will not transcribe the descriptions of Gomara, Benzoni and Herrera, as they wrote a long time after his death, and did nothing more than copy from Peter Martyr, Oviedo, Las Casas and Fernando.

Any picture not agreeing with these descriptions, must be immediately rejected as apocryphal and absolutely worthless.

FIRST GROUP.

I consider as belonging to the first group, that is to say to the pictures or engravings, the originals of which were, perhaps, taken from life at different periods of the Admiral's career, the following, namely :

I. The original of the engraving published in the illustrated edition of the works of Paulus Jovius. This was taken from a picture in the Jovian Gallery, which was there before 1546. A copy of the same picture made before the year 1568, is in the Uffizi Gallery in Florence. There are many pretended originals of this Jovian picture :

    1—The portrait at Como, known as the de Orchi.

    2—The picture at the National Library, Madrid, known as the Yañez portrait.

    3—The Cogoletto portrait.

    4—The Cuccaro portrait, from which was taken the Cancellieri medallion.

II. The original of the engraving published by Capriolo.

III. The picture attributed to Antonio del Rincon.

IV. The Juan de la Cosa portrait.

V. The Lotto portrait.

VI. The miniature in the Cluny Museum at Paris, from which, perhaps, the portrait by Sir Anthony More was taken.

And all the pictures taken with more or less fidelity from the above-mentioned. I will now proceed to describe them.

I. THE JOVIUS PORTRAIT.

Paulus Jovius, or Paolo Giovio, Archbishop of Nocera, was born in 1483, and died in 1552.

Jovius published in 1592, at Florence, a book called *Elogia Virorum Bellicâ Virtute Illustrium,* in which is found a eulogy of Columbus. This edition, notwithstanding the authoritative opinion of Harrisse, had no engravings. There is another edition of 1551, which I have not succeeded in finding, but Winsor says (*II. 72*,) that it has no engravings, and that it gives an account of Columbus on *p. 171;* but the third edition of the said book, published at Basle in 1575, was full of engravings. Among them is the one which I copy. In the third edition the wood engravings were by Tobias Stimmer, a native of Schaffhausen, and the same portrait is found in it.

In order to show the paramount importance of this portrait it will be necessary to enter into some details regarding the illustrious collector of the gallery.

Jovius was born at Como, Lombardy, on April 19th, 1483, and died at Florence, on December 11th, 1552. He studied at the great University of Pavia, from which he graduated as a physician, with the highest honors. Having much love for geographical and historical studies and also for natural history, he abandoned medicine and applied himself to literature. He was a man without conscience or principles, mendacious, a flatterer, calumniator and intriguer, but of brilliant talents, extensive knowledge, untiring activity, and of great artistic taste. Thanks to these high qualifications, he soon won eminence at the Pontifical Court and attained the position of Archbishop of Nocera. His works became famous in his time, but as his venal pen never hesitated in writing in favor of the highest bidder, he is at present absolutely discredited as a historian.

Jovius amassed an immense fortune; and his knowledge, his artistic tastes and his venality, placed him in close personal relations with the foremost representative men of his time. Eight enormous volumes have been published containing a portion of his correspondence with a very large number of persons distinguished in arms, sciences, literature and arts, among whom were Emperor Charles V., King Henry II., Popes Clement VII., Julius II., Leo X., and Paul III., the Constable de Montmorenci, the Duke of Alba, and Cardinals Farnesi and Guise.

He wrote a large number of volumes on many subjects, and in his famous villa on the shore of the Lake of Como, he collected a splendid library, a beautiful cabinet of antiquities, and finally a superb gallery of portraits of famous men. These have won for him an immortality which he did not deserve, on account of his vices and immorality.

On the same spot where the villa of Pliny the Younger once stood near Lake Como, Jovius built his house, a part of which yet remains. He formed his large collection of portraits of famous persons at an immense expense. Those of all his contemporaries were taken from life by the most distinguished

artists; and his collection acquired such great importance and favor that
so noble a genius as Julius Romanus bequeathed to it, in 1547, a superb
collection of portraits, the work of Raphael, for he believed "he could not
find a better place for them." Many artists sent their works there because
they considered it an honor to be represented in that famous gallery. About
the year 1550 the Duke of Tuscany sent Christopher dell'Altissimo and other
painters there, to take copies of them for the Florence Gallery; and we know
that before 1568 two hundred and eighty of these copies were hanging there,
because Vasari mentions them on that date, and among those portraits he
includes that of Columbus under No. 6 of the series of "Heroes." This
portrait is yet hanging in the Gallery and is numbered 397. In the Vasari
Catalogue it is properly placed between Vespucci and Magellan.

The correspondence of Jovius gives the fullest evidence of his strenuous
efforts and great expenditures to obtain trustworthy portraits of the persons
he wanted to place in his gallery. He was a fanatical and enthusiastic believer
in Columbus, to whom he wanted to erect a magnificent statue. It is not
credible that he would be satisfied with an imaginary copy of the features
of his great fellow-citizen, nor is it likely that he should have ordered a
portrait of the Admiral from life, as he was only twenty-three years old at the
time of the death of Columbus. Therefore we are bound to believe that he
did not hesitate to acquire, at any price, some trustworthy portrait of the
Admiral taken from life, either by some Spanish painter or by one of the
many Italian artists who were then traveling through Spain.

Years after the death of Jovius a large part of this gallery was distributed
among the different branches of his family, and although a great number of
his pictures are yet kept in the same place, unluckily that of Columbus is not
among them, and it is not known where it can be found. Some persons
pretend that the picture at Madrid, known as the Yañez portrait, is that
original; others that it is the De Orchi picture. I will speak hereinafter about
these; but I must state thus early that none of them can be either the original
of the engraving in the work of Jovius, or in that of Capriolo, nor the original
of the famous and well-authenticated copy in the Uffizi Gallery at Florence,
which is positively known to have been taken from the Como picture.

I agree with an illustrious Spanish writer, Cayetano Rossell, who says:
"In my opinion, it is incontrovertible that Jovius obtained somewhere an
authentic portrait of the Discoverer of the New World." This is proven by
the copy made for the Uffizi Gallery, by tradition, and by the assertion of the
editor of the work of Jovius, who reproduced all the pictures found in the
museum of Jovius, and says: "I have at much expense employed an eminent

artist to engrave Jovian portraits painted from life." Furthermore, we are led to believe it by the personal importance of Jovius himself.

As Jovius had personal relations with the Emperor Charles V. and with many distinguished Spaniards, nothing could be easier than for him to obtain either an original portrait from life or a copy of the same, by an artist at the court of Spain, perhaps by Antonio del Rincon, who undoubtedly knew Columbus personally, as he died in 1500, and who during the last years of his life was always at court, having been appointed royal painter by the Catholic kings many years before.

The importance of this original picture being thus explained, I will proceed to describe the cut taken from it, which is the first portrait of Columbus ever published.

The engraving is on wood and somewhat rough, but full of vigor and life, as is almost every one in

2.—THE JOVIUS PORTRAIT.

the book. It is a copy taken from the edition of the *Elogia* of 1575, which I owe to the kindness of the well-known Americanist, ex-Chief Justice Charles P. Daly. It represents Columbus at over fifty years of age, with abundant and curly hair, without beard or mustache. It is a half-length, showing the hands. The dress looks, at first sight, like that of a monk, but I believe, with Messrs. Carderera and Rios, that it is simply the old Spanish tabard, a kind of cloak worn in Spain in the most ancient times, and still in use by the sailors of the Bay of Biscay. (See frontispiece.)

This engraving, with some more or less slight changes, has been reproduced in a great number of books. I also give another cut of it, slightly different in treatment, because the features are clearer and more expressive than in the first. (Cut No. 2.)

The most important copy of the Jovian portrait is undoubtedly that in the Uffizi Gallery, Florence. It has been there, as I stated above, prior to the year 1568, and was probably painted by l'Altissimo. But whoever the painter be who executed this copy he was not a faithful copyist. He deliberately tried to soften the harsh features of the weather-beaten mariner, and made the expression milder, representing the face as fuller and the lineaments less

3.—THE FLORENCE PORTRAIT.

prominent, but in so doing he took away the energy and vigor, and the expression of decision which is so remarkable in Jovius' book. The painter who made the Jefferson copy tried to soften it still more, and his picture has no expression at all.

Cut No. 3 is a copy of the portrait in the Uffizi Gallery. It was certainly there before 1567, and probably since 1552; therefore it is the oldest perfectly-authenticated picture of Columbus.

Many copies in oil have been taken from this one. Among them that owned by Jefferson, and now in the Library of the Massachusetts Historical Society, is very well known. It has also been copied by all kinds of processes. I have in my possession over twenty copies of this picture. One is a photograph directly from the one at Florence. All are widely different, and are a good proof of the little reliance to be placed upon copies.

The engraving in the Jovius book and the Florence portrait may be considered as the originals of about all the pictures of any importance. Artists have introduced sundry variations in them; some deliberately, to make people believe they were originals or copies from unknown originals, some from a want of skill, but in the greater part of them it is easy to detect that they all represent one single type—that of Jovius.

2. THE YAÑEZ PORTRAIT,

PRETENDED BY MANY TO BE THE ORIGINAL PICTURE IN THE JOVIUS GALLERY

This picture is of the highest importance, and deserves, therefore, to be carefully considered.

In the year 1763, the Spanish Government bought from Mr. Yañez, a resident of Granada, a set of four beautiful though somewhat dilapidated portraits, representing Columbus, Cortés, Quevedo and Lope de Vega. Judging from appearances all were painted by the same hand; and those of Cortés Quevedo and Lope are excellent likenesses. This precludes all idea that the Columbus portrait could have been taken from life, as Cortés was almost a boy when Columbus died, and Quevedo and Lope were born almost half a century after his death.

This portrait remained for long years in a corner of the Royal (now National) Library, and until the time of Navarrete, about the beginning of this century, nobody paid any attention to it; but Navarrete, after a careful examination, attached great importance to this picture and always showed a great predilection for it.

Carderera says: "The picture is two feet high, painted on a poplar-wood board (*chopo*), a wood which was never used by the Spanish artists of that time, though it was much employed by the Italians. It is the same size as the Jovian picture, and has the same epigraph; the painter, besides, was a mannerist and wielded a weak brush. The fur robe, close-fitting and crossed in the front, differs widely from that in all known pictures; but a

4—THE YAÑEZ PORTRAIT, AS PURCHASED.

scrupulous examination has convinced me that it is recent, and the work of a modern restorer. It looks like an alteration made a few years ago by inexpert hands."

In Cut No. 4 I present this picture as it appeared before 1877. I will only add that Carderera considers it an old copy of the Jovian picture, and as the oldest portrait of Columbus existing in Spain. He believes it was painted in Italy in the sixteenth century by some artist of the Florentine school.

On petition of Mr. Carderera and other artists, who made an interesting

5—THE YAÑEZ PORTRAIT, AS IT NOW APPEARS.

report about this picture, it was decided to try to discover if, under the clumsy brush marks of the modern restorer, the original lines could be found; and never was an operation of this kind performed with greater success.

Following the instructions of Carderera, and under the direction of the distinguished Librarian of the National Library, the able artist, Mr. Salvador Martinez Cubells, undertook this delicate task. The first order received by him was simply "to make an examination, and if from it it was found with certainty that the original had received arbitrary touches of the brush defacing it, to re-establish, as far as possible, all that had disappeared in the drawing and in the coloring." Mr. Cubells began at the top of the picture, and saw immediately that the legend had been changed, and that where he found "CRISTOF COLUMBUS, NORI (sic) ORBIS INVENTOR," the old epigraph read, "COLUMBUS LYGUR. NOVI ORBIS REPTOR." In view of this, he continued cleaning off all the traces of the restoration, and under the old picture he found a new one full of life and vigor, which has all the characteristics of Columbus and bears an extraordinary resemblance to the Jovian type. This was beautifully engraved by José Maria Galvan, and from that engraving is taken the cut which I reproduce. (Cut No. 5.)

The picture had been examined, after its resuscitation, by a great number of artists and experts, who are all of opinion that it does not belong to the Spanish School, as the style and the coloring are that of the Florentine—that of the Altissimo ; that it may have been painted by some one of the disciples of the Bronzino ; and that there is no doubt that it was painted in Italy in the sixteenth century.

Mr. Rosell adds: "It is useless to state more reasons in favor of the authenticity of this portrait, which, after having been cleaned, gives evidence that it is one of the oldest known, and which by its material, form, features, dress and other conditions, offers greater proof of genuineness than any other of those found in our private galleries."

A comparison of the picture in its first and second states will show at a glance the wide difference between them and the clumsiness of the dauber who pretended to restore it.

Mr. Rios claims that this is the original Jovius picture, but I do not consider his reasons of sufficient weight to disprove the fact that the four pictures purchased together appear to be from the same hand, which shows that they could not have been painted prior to the last years of the sixteenth century.

In this picture the hair is shorter than in the portrait at Florence and in the Capriolo cut, but is similar to the cut in Jovius' book.

It is a curious fact that not a portrait of Columbus is found in any of the catalogues of the collections of the Kings of Spain, from Philip II. to Philip V.

This Yañez portrait, as it now stands, is perhaps the only one in which are

presented complete all the characteristics of Columbus, as described by those
who knew him personally.   It is to be regretted that it was not painted by a

6—THE COGOLETTO PORTRAIT.

first-rate artist, and that it is not possible to obtain its full history before it
was bought for the Royal Library.

General Fairchild presented a copy of this portrait to the Historical
Society of Wisconsin, a few years ago.

Cogoletto is a small village fifteen miles from Genoa, which claims to be

the birthplace of Christopher Columbus   A tablet has been placed in an
old house in one of the principal streets in commemoration of this dubious

7—THE DE ORCHI PORTRAIT.

fact.   Nevertheless, the very room and the corner in which the Discoverer
was born are shown to all visitors who are willing to spend a small sum for the
privilege of admission.   In this house there is also a small portrait of

Columbus which is asserted to be of great antiquity, but evidently it is only a copy from the Jovius.

But there is another picture in the Council Hall of the village which is really deeply interesting. Its antiquity has been almost proven by Isnardi in his work, *Sulle Patria de Colombo*, who says that its history can be traced for over three hundred years; and some have gone so far as to pretend that it is the original and now lost portrait of the Jovian Gallery. A single glance at it will show its striking likeness to the Altissimo, to the de Orchi and the Yañez portraits, and to all those emanating from the Jovian type. (See Cut No. 6.) It even has the same inscription, thus showing their common origin. The picture is in bad condition, and does not appear to be the work of a master-hand.

There is a picture at Cuccaro, in the house of Fidele Guglielmo Colombo, which has been preserved for long years by the branch of the Colombo family residing in this place. Cuccaro also claims to be the birthplace of Columbus, and the family asserts in addition that this is the original Jovius portrait, but according to experts it is only a poor copy of it. Napione accepted this picture as genuine; Cancellieri was of the same opinion, and copied and engraved it in his work.

Feuillet de Conches says that there is another portrait in the Castle of Cuccaro, and that this is only a copy of the Florence portrait.

Another picture which, not only on account of its intrinsic artistic merit, but also because the owner pretends that it is the original Jovian portrait, is deserving of an extended notice; I refer to the one belonging to Count de Orchi, which is shown in Cut No. 7.

A slight examination will show that this picture and the one in the Uffizi Gallery of Florence have undoubtedly a common origin. The following data about the history of this picture I owe to my distinguished friend and relative, Mr. José S. Jorrin, of Havana, who has written many able essays on Columbus, but, unfortunately for Cuban literature, has not yet published his very complete life of the great Admiral, to which he has devoted many years of his useful life.

Mr. Jorrin, in one of his trips to Italy, became acquainted with Count Giovanni Giovio, the only member of the family of the famous Bishop of Nocera who bears that historical name, and from a long correspondence which was carried on between them, from March 7th, 1879, to April 6th, 1880, he obtained the following facts:

"Many of the pictures of the said Jovian Museum remain yet at Como, in the old home of the founder, which is still called *Edes Jovis*.

"The collection was divided, a long time ago, between the two branches of the family which were the principal heirs, one taking the pictures of men illustrious in arms, the other that of men illustrious in letters.

"The first branch is represented at present by the Marquis Giorgio Raimondi, the noble family de Orchi and Mr. Vietro Novelli; the second by Count Francisco and three nieces.

"The family de Orchi sold to Prince Jérome Napoleon the portrait of Cosmo di Medici, painted by Bronzino, and it is the present owner of that of Columbus. On the upper part there is an inscription in two lines, 'COLUMBUS LYGUR., NOV. ORBIS REPTOR,' but its bad condition prevented a photograph being taken from it; therefore Count Giovanni Giovio requested the Milanese artist, Nessi, to make a very faithful and exact reproduction of it in crayon one-half the actual size. This drawing was photographed, and Mr. Jorrin obtained some copies of it."

Dr. Alessandro de Orchi is the present owner of this picture, which is not signed. Some attribute it to Bartolomeo Suardi and others to Sebastian del Piombo. If it was painted by Piombo it could not have been taken from life, as this artist was born in 1485, and therefore was only twenty-one years of age at the date of the death of Columbus in 1506, and he never left Italy until 1510.

Bartolomeo Suardi (*Il Bramantino*) reached the zenith of his fame at the end of the fifteenth century, and died in 1530; but there is no record of his having ever been in Spain, although we have very full accounts of his life.

The picture may be from the brush of one of these painters, or from that of any other distinguished artist, who, perhaps, copied it from an original Spanish painting, but its likeness to the Jovian cut and to the copy in the Uffizi Gallery is very remarkable, and the best judges ascribe it to a master hand.

The distinguished Americanist, Mr. Clement Markham, considers this picture as the only authentic portrait of Columbus now in existence.

I will now proceed to give a cursory description of the most important portraits based on the Jovian type, which are, the Belvedere, the Cancellieri, Crispin de Pas, Borghese, Malpica, Altamira, Villafranca and Talleyrand.

Another well-known copy of the Jovius picture is the Belvedere. It was painted in 1579, by order of Ferdinand I. of Austria, and in 1610 it became

8—THE BELVEDERE PORTRAIT.

the property of his son, Archduke Ferdinand, Count of Tyrol, who placed it in his castle of Ambras, near Innspruck, where it remained up to 1805, when it was taken to Vienna and placed in the Belvedere Gallery, where it can still be seen.

It is a beautiful, small miniature in oil, painted on wood, but the name of the eminent artist is unfortunately unknown. There is an engraving of it in *Frankl. Christoforo Colombo*, a German poem, published at Stuttgart in

1836. My cut No. 8 is taken from a lithograph, for which I am indebted to the kindness of ex-Chief Justice C. P. Daly.

Francesco de Cancellieri published a book at Rome, in 1809, with two title pages, the second of which reads, *Notizie Storiche e Bibliographiche di Christoforo Colombo di Cuccaro nel Mon-*

9—THE CANCELLIERI ENGRAVING.

ferrato, which is full of curious and interesting references to Columbus, who, as he claims, was born at Cuccaro.

On this title page there is a beautiful copper medallion, which Cancellieri says (*p. 180*) is taken from an old picture belonging to Fedele Guglielmo Colombo of Cuccaro, and engraved by Giuseppe Colendo (although it is signed *Joan Petrini sculpsit*), and which he prefers to any other, because "it must be the most faithful and correct likeness, since it has been for long years in the possession of the relatives of Columbus." The engraving is so small (Cut No. 9) that it is difficult to make much out of it; yet, at first sight, it appears to be a somewhat softened reproduction of the Capriolo engraving. It also looks very much like the one in the National Library and the Yañez portrait.

Carderera valued this little medallion very much on account of its artistic merit, but, as Cancellieri says, it is only a copy from the portrait of Cuccaro, which is taken from the portrait at the Jovian Gallery, and, therefore, has no claim to originality.

In a work entitled *Effigies Regum et Principum quorum Vis ac Potentia in Re Nautica seu Marina, præ cæteris Spectabilis est,* which was published at Cologne in 1598, is the beautiful portrait of Columbus, reproduced in cut 10, and for which I am indebted to the kindness of Mr. W. C. Curtis.

It is the work of the famous engraver, Crispin de Pas or de Passe. It is undoubtedly taken from Jovius, but is a far more artistic work than the Jovius or the Capriolo, and has greater deviations from the type. The attire is that of a Franciscan monk with the cowl, and a gold chain around the neck, and it holds a sextant in the left hand. The nose has been greatly changed, being no longer of the aquiline type; the hair is short and curled; but the features generally are those of the Jovius.

Carderera strongly criticizes the engraver who so arbitrarily deviated from the well-known type.

The chain is the one given to Columbus by the Cacique Guacanagari in Hispaniola, and to which Bernaldez refers in his history of the Catholic Kings.

In the Borghese Gallery there is a pretended portrait of Columbus, which it is claimed was painted in 1519. This painting is nothing more than a very unfaithful copy of the Jovius, and the date at which it was painted is not certainly known, but it is well-established that it is very old, and though there is no record of the name of the artist, it is undoubtedly the work of a master-hand.

According to Carderera, this is a copy painted by order of Prince Aldobrandini, and was for many years the ornament of his magnificent palace in Rome.

Some critics pretend that this picture is simply a representation of the Saviour which has been copied for the purpose of passing it off as a portrait of Columbus, yet the reputation of the gallery where it has been for so long does not permit of such a supposition.

10—THE CRISPIN DE PAS ENGRAVING.

In the gallery of the Marquis de Malpica at Madrid, where it was examined by Carderera and Rosell at their leisure, there was many years ago a picture of the Admiral. It has strangely disappeared, and it has been impossible to discover the slightest trace of its present whereabouts.

Mr. Carderera calls it a somewhat imperfect copy of the one in the Uffizi Gallery, with some minor alterations. It is a canvas two feet in height, presenting only the bust of Columbus, wearing a vest, over which is an ample dark green mantle. On the top is the epigraph, "CHRISTOFORUS LIGUR., NOVI ORBIS REPERTOR." Carderera believes the picture to be about three centuries old, and this is also the opinion of Rosell.

The Marquis of Villafranca, in 1601, collected a gallery of portraits of illustrious persons; and from a curious letter quoted by Carderera, I find that his agent in Rome wrote him "that the pictures of the Emperors are all finished, one hundred and fifty-seven in number, and that those of the illustrious men are completed with the exception of fifty, and that there will be in all three hundred and twenty pictures." Carderera says that he believes that all these pictures were copied from those that he had seen in Rome in the Borghese Palace, which were copied from those in the Jovian Museum; therefore, the portrait of Columbus in this gallery was simply a copy of the Jovius.

The picture in the gallery of the Count of Altamira was also a copy from that in the Uffizi Gallery. The collections in the palaces of Altamira and Villafranca have been dispersed, and the present whereabouts of these portraits of Columbus is unknown.

The Duke de Talleyrand, Sagan and Valençay has sent to the French Geographical Society at Paris a photographic copy of a pretended picture of Columbus. This picture belonged to the gallery of the famous diplomatist, Prince C. M. Talleyrand, and is now at the Chateau de Valençay, Département de L'Indre, France. The painting is very old and bears the following inscription:

"HÆC EST EFFIGIES LIGURI MIRANDI COLOMBI,
ANTIPODUM PRIMUS RATE QUI PENETRAVIT IN ORBEM,"

and the name of Sebastian del Piombo without any date. I have already given a notice of Piombo in the description of the de Orchi portrait.

Count Louis de Turenne, in a report to the French Academy, mentions that the picture is not only that of Columbus, painted by Sebastian del Piombo, but also that it is taken from life. Following the example of Roselly des Lorgues, he does not take the trouble of explaining from whence he derived his information.

I have not seen any engraving of it, but, from the descriptions which I have read, I suppose this portrait is only an old copy of the Altissimo, with some slight alterations.

THE CAPRIOLO PORTRAIT.

The engraving by Aliprando Capriolo was first published in the work, *Cento Capitani Illustri*, printed at Rome, in 1596; a second edition appeared in 1606, with additions by F. Tomasini.

The artistic work is greatly superior to that of Jovius, but there is no doubt that the picture in the Jovian Gallery was the original of the Capriolo,

11—THE CAPRIOLO ENGRAVING.

although many variations were introduced in it, owing in part to the faulty style of Capriolo, who always wanted to represent all his heroes as good-looking, and, with that end in view, purposely softened the vigorous lineaments, depriving his pictures of energy and life.

The portrait is a bust, with long lank hair, carefully combed at the sides and covering the ears. The tabard is changed to a Roman toga, crossed over the shoulders, and in a corner are seen the arms of Columbus. Carderera considered the engraving as one of the most important portraits of Columbus, and was of opinion that this cut and that of Jovius were the most fitting to be used in erecting any iconographic monument to Columbus.

The illustrious Spanish writer Martin Fernandez de Navarrete also held this engraving in high esteem, and reproduced it in the French edition of one of his works.

The picture attributed to Rincon also bears an extraordinary resemblance to this Capriolo cut, which proves their common origin. ·

Carderera also states that a copy in oil of the Capriolo portrait has long been in the Uffizi Gallery.

The portrait in the Naval Museum at Madrid is nothing more than a splendid reproduction in oil of the Capriolo engraving and of other historical types. Mr. Curtis, in his able article already quoted, says: "It is asserted to be a genuine portrait painted in 1504 or 1505, in Seville, upon the return of Columbus from his fourth and last voyage, and shortly before his death ;"

and, with his usual good judgment, he adds, "but there is no evidence to
sustain the claim." I will say more: it is positively known that it was

12—PORTRAIT IN THE NAVAL MUSEUM, MADRID.

painted by order of the government, in 1838, by a French artist named Charles
Legrand, and only in French and American works have I seen the assertion to
which Mr. Curtis refers.

Carderera says: "We can but praise the judgment of the artist who, when called upon a few years ago to paint a portrait of Columbus for the Naval Museum, took as a model Capriolo's engraving. We disapprove of the change

13—THE CEVASCO PORTRAIT.

that the painter made in the dress, in copying the velvet cloak of the portrait in the National Library."

The picture in question is really beautiful; the expression of melancholy, benevolence and energy, and its exact agreement with the known traits of the physiognomy of Columbus, have rendered this portrait a universal favorite, and it is, as Mr. Curtis says, "one of the most widely known and generally accepted portraits of Columbus."

Many writers claim that it is a copy of the Jovius made in the sixteenth century—some going so far as to assert that it is the original itself. Others attribute it to Maella, but there is another portrait of Columbus from the brush of this able artist, and it differs so widely from the one in the Naval Museum that it is clearly seen that they cannot be the work of the same hand.

There is a beautiful copy of this portrait in the Geographical Society of New York, presented years ago by its enthusiastic President, ex-Chief-Justice Charles P. Daly.

In the Red Room of the Council Hall at Genoa there is an oil painting of Columbus, which was presented, in 1862, to the Municipality by the sculptor, G. B. Cevasco. I have not been able to obtain any details regarding the history of this painting, which is undoubtedly modern, but I have secured a copy of it, which I reproduce in cut No. 13.

I believe it is an imitation of the picture in the Naval Museum with some variations, taken, perhaps, from Capriolo. The face is full of energy and intelligence, and the dress is the conventional one. The hair is long and flowing, and is almost covered by a barret-cap. The artist was not a common one, and has followed the well-known descriptions of the Admiral.

In the splendid work entitled *Iconographie di Uomini Sommi nelle Scienze e nelle Arti Italiani*, Naples, 1854, there is a beautiful engraving of a portrait in oil by Stuppi. I believe Mr. Curtis was

14—THE CANTU ENGRAVING.

perfectly right in saying that " it is undoubtedly a copy of the Capriolo
engraving," but I may add that the artist did not improve on his model by
softening the austere lineaments of the Admiral.

Cut No. 14 is the reproduction of a steel engraving in *César Cantú,
Universal History*, the Spanish translation of which was published at Madrid
in 1856.

I believe that the artist followed the Capriolo, but he introduced so many
changes in it, that although it agrees with the general characteristics of
Columbus, yet there is a material difference between it and the Jovius and
Capriolo types.   The artist has greatly idealized the rough sketches of Jovius
and Capriolo, but at the same time has succeeded in presenting something
that may be accepted as a portrait of the Navigator.

III. THE ANTONIO DEL RINCON PORTRAIT.

This would be the most important portrait of Columbus, if its authenticity
could be established.   It tallies exactly with the descriptions of the Admiral,
and looks very much like the Jovian portrait.   It is very old, and has been
reproduced numberless times.   From time immemorial it has been in the
private library of the Kings of Spain, and it is said traditionally that it was
painted by Antonio del Rincon upon the return of Columbus from his second
voyage.

Unfortunately, there is not a scintilla of evidence as to its authenticity.   It
is not even known when or how it became the property of the Crown, as
neither Palomino, Pacheco, nor Cean Bermudez mentions this portrait among
the known works of this artist.

Notwithstanding this fact the picture is very old, and was evidently the
work of a great artist.   Copies of it were taken and published before 1600,
and its general characteristics confirm the belief that it is an original Rincon,
or, if not, it is at least the work of one of his disciples.

There are many reasons advanced to show that Rincon painted a picture
of Columbus.   Rincon, who was the true father of the Spanish School of
Painting, was born at Guadalajara in 1446, and died at Seville in 1500.   He

was for years court painter to Ferdinand and Isabella, whose portraits he painted; and they were still in the Church of San Juan de los Reyes, at Toledo, when Palomino wrote his *Historia de la Pintura en España*, Vol. *II.*, *p.* 235. He also painted some portraits of Princes, and that of Antonio de Nebrija. He resided at court from 1493 up to his death in 1500, and must have become acquainted with Columbus upon his return from his first voyage. It is therefore almost incredible that he should not have painted a portrait of the Discoverer, either by command of the Kings or by request of the Admiral himself, who was a very vain-glorious man, and then in the zenith of his fame. Furthermore the p o r t r a i t, though exceedingly old, has such a spirited air, and such a vigorous expression, that it

15—THE RINCON PORTRAIT.

looks exactly as though it were taken directly from life. Even the serene expression of the face appears to indicate that this portrait was taken during the few months in which the Admiral led a happy life. (Cut No. 15.)

There were at one time in Spain many pictures by this artist, all belonging to the Crown; but most of them were destroyed in the terrible conflagration at the royal residence, El Pardo, in 1608, together with a large number of the works of other early Spanish artists. Yet I must say that in the catalogue of El Pardo there is no mention of any portrait of Columbus by Rincon, or by any other master; and, besides that, there is no mention of Columbus ever having sat before the easel of Rincon.

The medallion painted by Julio Romano has a great resemblance to this painting. This type was very well known outside of Spain at a very early period, and was reproduced, with some changes, in foreign editions of Herrera, in Van der Aa, and in many other books.

Roselly des Lorgues has also accepted and published this picture in his
"*Life of Columbus*," and he has in his collection the portrait in oil, from
which he took his engraving, and claims that his painting is the original work
of Rincon. But the good old Count has gone so far in many points, referring
to St. Christopher Columbus, that we must not place much faith in his new
claim. He has also presented to the astonished reader a portrait of Beatriz
Enriquez, the noble Cordovan lady, mother of Ferdinand Columbus. Where
did he obtain it? And what proof has he of its being genuine? These are
idle questions. It is well known that the apologist of the "*Bearer of the
Cross*" never paid much attention to evidence of any kind. Yet I cannot but
approve his selection of this portrait for his book, as this is perhaps the only
plausible assumption in all his alleged discoveries about Columbus.

The Navarrete portrait, as can be seen at a glance, is a copy of the Rincon,
with, perhaps, some minor changes taken from the Capriolo picture. The

artist has changed the position, and the
Admiral is represented as looking to the
left. It was published in the Parisian
edition of Navarrete's work, *Relation des
Quatre Voyages de Christophe Colomb*,
(1828). Mr. Curtis believes it is taken
from the picture in the Naval Museum,
which it resembles in some general traits
and in the position of the head. It bears
a curious note which reads: "Engraved
on stone by Pedro Colon, Duke of Vera-
guas, a descendant of the illustrious navigator, and is taken from an original and
contemporary portrait which once belong-

16—THE NAVARRETE PORTRAIT.

ed to his Catholic Majesty." This shows with certainty that it is a copy from
the Rincon.

In the splendid edition of the *Codice Diplomatico Colombino*, published by
Banchero, in Genoa, there is a lithograph representing Columbus which is
evidently taken from the Rincon portrait, with the exception of some slight
variations in the shape of the mouth. I reproduce this picture not only on
account of its beauty, but also to show the high esteem in which the Rincon
portrait is held, not only in Spain and France, but in Italy as well. (Cut
No. 17.)

As the best description I have found of the two portraits in the Museum of
Rouen, France, is that given by Mr. Curtis in the *Cosmopolitan Magazine*,

I will take the liberty of copying it verbatim from his article: "In the Museum at Rouen, France, are two pictures of Columbus, placed side by side, but as unlike as it is possible for two portraits of the same person

17—THE BANCHERO PORTRAIT.

to be, and the contrast is very amusing. In one the hair is gray and thin, and the flesh is pallid. It is a modern canvas, signed P. Le Carpentier, and inscribed, 'COLUMBUS LIGUR. NOVI ORBIS REPTOR.' A note on the back says: 'This portrait was copied in wax in 1835 from the original portrait of Sebastian del Piombo, which formed a part of the collection of the Escurial, and which is attributed by some to Antonio del Rincon.' It is evidently a copy of the portrait in the Queen's Library at Madrid.

"The other Rouen portrait is a sharp and vigorous piece of work, with black hair, black eyes, considerable color and expressive features. It points a finger to a sphere resting upon a table with some books."

IV. THE JUAN DE LA COSA PORTRAIT.

The famous chart of Juan de la Cosa, the pilot of Columbus, is drawn on parchment and bears an inscription which reads, "*Juan de la Cosa la fizo en el puerto de Santa Maria en el año 1500.*" This chart, which was first described in the most eulogistic terms by Humboldt, was then the property of Baron Walckenaer, and is now in the Naval Museum at Madrid.

On one of its sides, in the place that would correspond to the position of Mexico and Central America, there is a miniature representing St. Christopher conveying the Infant Jesus on his back from one continent to the other. The drawing is rude, and the features of the Saint have not the slightest resemblance to those of Columbus, as described by his contemporaries. There is no direct evidence to show that Juan de la Cosa ever intended to portray Columbus in this chart, yet I doubt not that La Cosa may have tried to depict in it the allegorical representation of his chief (whose name signifies "Christ-Bearer") under the figure of this saint carrying the Christ on his shoulders, though St. Christopher was never considered as a patron of navigators; and that in doing this he never intended to present a faithful portrait of the Admiral. That is entirely in accordance with the customs of those times, as can be seen by the delineations of many kings represented in the same chart, none of which are claimed to be portraits.

One of the defenders of this picture is Roselly des Lorgues, who considers it symbolical of the discoveries of Columbus and of his purpose to extend the Catholic religion. Winsor says that some authors claim that the picture of Herrera is based on that of Juan de la Cosa. I quite agree with him when he says: "This theory is hardly accepted by the critics."

I present to my readers this picture, which is taken from the new copy of the map of La Cosa, published at Madrid, not only as a pretended portrait of Columbus, but also as a very curious and interesting historical allegory. In

18—THE JUAN DE LA COSA PORTRAIT.

fact, though it looks more like a grotesque Japanese caricature than a Spanish
picture of the year 1500, its genuineness is unquestionable, and it is the
earliest attempt known to portray Columbus, if such was the intention of the
famous pilot.

V. THE LOTTO PORTRAIT.

This is undoubtedly one of the most important portraits of Columbus. It
is a beautiful work of art, is signed "Laurens Lotto F. 1512," and the most
distinguished experts, as Bode, Raineri, Morelli, Cavalcasette, and others, are
of the opinion that there is no doubt about its being a work of the famous
master. Therefore I will raise no doubt as to its antiquity and authenticity,
as coming from the brush of Lotto. But does it represent Columbus? and, if
so, was it, as is claimed, taken from life?

Mr. John C. Van Dyke has published in the *Century Magazine* (October
1892), an admirable article about this now famous picture. In view of its
comprehensiveness, fairness and sound reasoning, I will take the liberty of
quoting from it somewhat freely.

The history of this picture after it was painted is thus given in the article:

"It is supposed to have been painted for Domenico Malipiero, the
Venetian Senator and historian, at the instance of his correspondent, Angelo
Trevisan (Trivigiano), secretary of the Venetian ambassador to Spain, who in
1501 was in intimate communication with Christopher Columbus at Granada.
Malipiero's manuscripts (and possibly this picture) are said to have passed to
Senator Francesco Longo. The Gradenigos were the heirs of the Longos, and
it was from them that the Cavaliere Luigi Rossi, a steward of the Duchess of
Parma, purchased the picture. Just before Rossi's death the picture was
sold to a person named Gandolfi, who had it somewhat repaired and restored.
The badly damaged head and red cap of an Indian at the right were cut out,
and the picture was made square instead of oblong. From Gandolfi it passed
to Signor Antonio della Rovere, of Venice, in whose house it was seen in 1891,
by Captain Frederick H. Mason, United States Consul-General at Frankfort-
on-the-Main, and by him bought for the World's Fair at Chicago. The record
cannot be traced with any certainty beyond the Gradenigos, and even if it
could it would prove no more than what the picture itself reveals."

To all this I must add that the present owner of this picture is Mr. James
W. Ellsworth of Chicago, and for this reason it is often called "the Ellsworth
picture."

I will now describe this painting (cut No. 19), and, as I have never seen the original, I will make use of another able article, which I find in the *Progresso Italo-Americano* of this city, signed with the initials "P. S.," the writer of which is also an ardent admirer of the Lotto portrait.

The picture at present is three feet by two feet eight inches in size. Originally it was larger, but on account of careless handling it was so damaged

19—THE LOTTO (ELLSWORTH) PORTRAIT.

that it was found necessary to trim it to its present dimensions about the middle of this century. The face is turned to the right, as can be seen in the cut (No. 19). The head is uncovered, the hair white and falling almost to the shoulders; it is parted in the middle, and the face is clean shaven. The carnation is almost of a bronze color; and he is clothed in a low-necked white

shirt without collar, with a red or scarlet coat, which is almost concealed by
an ample mantle, with fur lapels, somewhat after the fashion of the one
in the Yañez portrait, before all the additions by an inexpert restorer were
removed. In the right hand he holds a chart copied from that by de
Ruysch, in 1508, and in the left a common nautical hour-glass, which
stands upon a book labelled *Aristotel*, and there are other books on the top
of a book-case. The background is gray, and in the right hand corner is
a window giving a view of a landscape. It is said that before the picture
was trimmed there was the head of an Indian in the foreground.

The map itself is sufficient evidence that the picture was not taken from
life, as it was first published in 1508, two years after Columbus' death, or
six or seven years subsequent to 1501 or 1502, when it is pretended that it was
painted. The able defence of this map by Mr. Van Dyke, who maintains that
all the countries shown in it were already known to the Spaniards, falls to the
ground when we consider the telling fact discovered by the keen eye of Mr.
Harrisse that the artist has copied the errors of longitude which are found in
the de Ruysch map.

I will not deny the possibility that some Italian or Spanish artist (and
there were many capable ones then in Spain, notwithstanding the assertion of
Mr. Van Dyke to the contrary), may have taken a picture of Columbus from
life, and that Lotto may have copied it, making, as was very common, some
more or less appropriate additions. But in any event, if the Lotto portrait
was ever intended to represent Columbus, it was not taken from life, and
therefore cannot be accepted as an archetype, as is claimed by its defenders.

I admit that the picture bears a certain resemblance to that in the Naval
Museum; but this is undoubtedly modern. I also admit that it has some of
the well-known characteristics of Columbus, but I cannot for a moment
agree with the opinion of Mr. Van Dyke, when he says, "a comparison,
feature by feature, will show that the Lotto portrait tallies exactly with the
descriptions that we have of Columbus.

I repeat that I have never seen the original picture. I have over twenty
copies of it, photographed, engraved and reproduced by different processes,
and some of them are splendid, but in none of them have I been able to find
"the air of authority," or "the appearance of a nobleman," and find that none
of them tally exactly with the descriptions in our possession of the person of
Columbus. I will say more: I find the face in the Lotto portrait vulgar and
wanting in energy, looking more like that of an old women than of a man
of the decided character, iron will, and clear intelligence of the great Admiral.
Perhaps I may change my opinion if I see the original portrait; possibly I may

see all the qualities that Mr. Van Dyke claims for it, but the copies in my possession, which, as I have said, number over twenty, do not give an idea of the Columbus whose description we now have.

I have already given the history of the picture after it was painted. I will now present to my readers the history of *how* it was painted, and will take it from Mr. Curtis' article:

"When the discoveries of Columbus became known in Venice, Dominico Pisano was sent as an embassador from that republic to the court of Spain. He went chiefly for the purpose of obtaining information for the use of the merchants of Venice concerning the commercial value, the resources and products of the newly discovered lands, and to obtain maps and charts for the benefit of Venetian navigators. He had a secretary named Giovanni Camerino, or Cietrico, who made it his business to cultivate Columbus and succeeded in becoming very intimate with him. Camerino obtained secretly from the discoverer a chart of the new world and sent it to Venice.

"Pisano also forwarded to his government many voluminous reports concerning the discoveries of Columbus, which were based upon information received directly from the Admiral and his companions on the voyages. It is known also that Lorenzo Lotto visited Spain while Pisano was there and completed several important works of art under his patronage. There are sixteen examples from his brush now in the city of Madrid, painted in Granada, Seville and other places during these years. While there is no record or tangible evidence that Columbus ever sat before his easel, it is very probable that he did so, as just at the time of his visit the Venetian ambassador was cultivating him with the most assiduous attentions and hospitality."

There is in Paris, *a certain troublesome American lawyer* who has almost consecrated his life to the study of early American history, who entertains no respect for fables, legends, traditions, or old woman's tales, has no love for romance in history, and is decidedly opposed to all those who *are striving to make a delusion and a farce of history.* As soon as he read the articles of Mr. Curtis and others, he took up his trenchant pen and sent a letter to the editor of the *Sun* of New York, from which we quote the following caustic paragraphs:

"It is not true that Domenico Pisani was sent to Spain as an ambassador from the Venetian Republic when the discoveries of Columbus became known in Venice.

"It is not true that he went chiefly or at all for the purpose of obtaining information for the use of the merchants of Venice concerning the commercial value, the resources and products of the newly discovered lands, and to obtain maps and charts for the benefit of the Venetian navigators.

"It is not true that Pisano 'had a secretary named Giovanni Camerino or Cietrico.'

"It is not true that the said Camerino, or Cietrico, 'obtained secretly from the discoverer a chart of the New World.'

"It is not true that 'Pisano forwarded to his government many voluminous reports concerning the discoveries of Columbus.'

"It is not true that 'Lorenzo Lotto visited Spain while Pisano was there, and completed several important works of art under his patronage.'

"It is not true that 'there are sixteen or any examples from his brush now in the city of Madrid, painted in Granada, Seville, and other places during these years.'

"It is not true that 'the history of the canvas may be traced back nearly three centuries.'

"As to the picture itself, viewed at least as a 'portrait of Christopher Columbus,' it is a sheer Italian fabrication, which, like all Italian forgeries, particularly those of Bolognese or of Venetian origin, proves too much."

"Columbus is made therein to hold a map. The map is not, as we should have supposed, a map of his maritime discoveries. It is a map of Brazil, which he never discovered, or claimed to have discovered, or visited at any time. It is not even a Spanish map."

Who is right in this question? Let the reader decide for himself. As for myself, I regret to state that however able the presentation of the claims, by Mr. Curtis, and however powerful the defence of it made by Mr. Van Dyke may be, and without disputing the authorship of this beautiful work of art, I feel inclined to repeat, with the scholarly author of so many admirable works of Columbus:

"Withal, it should be stated, in justice to the 'Lotto portrait of Columbus,' that it is neither better nor worse than any and all the other apocryphal daubs and portraits which are now being collected in Italy, in Spain, and in the United States, by over-zealous patriots, who do not seem to be aware that they are striving to make of history a delusion and a farce!"

VI. THE PICTURE IN THE MUSEUM AT CLUNY.

On page 272 of *Lecoy de la Marche, Les Manuscrits et la Miniature*, a beautiful work published by the *Bibliothèque de L'Enseignement des Beaux Arts*. Paris, without date, but about 1887, I find the following important notice:

"During the Renaissance, the painter Vasco, a disciple of Perugino, embellished a collection of documents deposited in the Portuguese Torre del Tombo, very richly with vignettes and arabesques. About the same time, a Spanish artist painted on parchment an interesting portrait of Christopher Columbus, *El Descubridor del Nuevo Mundo* (the Discoverer of the New World). It is a full face portrait, attired in a plaited shirt and a yellow doublet with stripes of various colors. The head is covered by an angular cap with turned up edges. This portrait can now be seen at the Museum at Cluny."

Perugino (Pietro Vannuci), the teacher of Raphael, was born in 1446. He opened his school at Perugia in 1490, and died there in 1524. Therefore, the Spanish artist who painted this miniature might very well have taken it from life. I have never seen a copy of this portrait, neither have I seen it mentioned in any book, but I consider it of the highest importance and deserving of very careful study.

Could this portrait be one of the two miniatures from which it is claimed that the Morus portrait was copied? The description does not agree, but Morus may have changed the dress and followed the features in the miniature.

THE SIR ANTHONY MORE PORTRAIT.

I am indebted to the kindness of Mr. Charles F. Gunther, of Chicago, not only for many photographic copies of this truly superb picture, one of which I reproduce, but also for many interesting notices about it.

Whilst I completely agree with the courteous owner of this artistic jewel in regard to its uncommon merits as a picture, I regret, nevertheless, to state that his arguments have failed to dispel from my mind the doubts that I have always entertained of its being a portrait of Columbus. The face undoubtedly has some of the well-known lineaments of the Admiral, but the most important are completely wanting—the long face, the high-cheek bones, the peculiar eyebrows, which are so characteristic of Columbus, could not have escaped the

20—THE SIR ANTHONY MORE (GUNTHER) PORTRAIT.

eye of such a man as Anthony More. I will not pay much attention to the absurd dress, which did not come into fashion until about a century later, because it is a well-settled fact that the artists of the sixteenth and seventeenth centuries were in the habit of attiring their heroes in any manner which suited their fancy, without regard to historical accuracy ; but I cannot accept as a portrait of Columbus, *copied from a miniature taken from life*, that face with the queerly cropped hair, mustache and goatee.

Mr. Curtis, in the *Cosmopolitan Magazine*, gives the following history of this painting : "This portrait of Columbus was painted about 1570, at the order of Margaret of Parma, from a miniature said to have been in the possession of the royal family at Madrid. The Gunther portrait was removed to Spain when the Spanish Court abandoned the Netherlands, and is said to have hung in the cabin of one of the vessels of the Spanish Armada during the famous sea fight of 1588. The vessel which carried it went to pieces on the Cornish coast of England, and the owner of the adjoining estate kept the picture as his share of the wreckage. From that date, to the middle of the present century it remained in the possession of the same family, when it was purchased by William Cribb, of Covent Garden, London. His descendants sold it to Mr. Gunther. The portrait was engraved in 1850, and was used by Irving to illustrate his life of Columbus. It is painted upon a panel of wood, about three feet by two in size, and bears in faint letters the inscription 'Ch. Colombo.' "

According to Mr. Gunther, " the allegorical frame in which the portrait is placed embodies one of the most remarkable and exquisite specimens of wood carving known of ancient or modern times. It is beautifully gilded, and is allegorical of the life of the discoverer, showing the drums, cannon, Indian arrows and armor of that period, capped with the Columbus coat of arms and its quarterings of oyster shells, swords, ship and anchor, and surmounted by a golden crown. It is carved in wood and is a master piece in its design and proportions, and illustrates such work as only royalty could command in that period."

" Upon the head of the drum carved in the frame is the date 1590, the year that the portrait was brought into England.

"The frame was made when the portrait was executed by Moro.

"The frame spoken of above, which was made at the same time as the portrait, is fully as interesting as the canvas. It is fashioned with superb skill and is a grand mass of intricate carving.

' It is gilded, and on the top there is the coat of arms and the quarterings of Columbus, the oyster shell, the anchor and the sword."

I repeat that I do not entertain any doubt about the authorship of this splendid work. According to the opinion of many experts, it is undoubtedly from the hand of Moro ; but did he intend in this portrait to represent Columbus ? The name in the corner is of no importance whatever.

The Jomard picture and many others which are entirely apocryphal show the same name.

The eminent Spanish painter and critic, Valentin Carderera, the author of the monumental works, *Iconografia Española*, and *Monumentos Arquitectónicos de España*, remarks very forcibly, " mustaches and goatees were *never worn* in the time of Columbus, and the hair, far from being cut short, was worn long and cut horizontally, very often covering the ears."

As Mr. Carderera's special field was the study of the old portraits and statues by Spanish artists, which he copied and published in his famous *Iconografia Española*, no man could be a better judge than he in the matter of the fashions prevailing at each period of the history of Spain.

Yet I would call the attention of the reader to what I say about the miniature in the Cluny Museum at Paris.

Mr. Gunther writes to me also in regard to some particular points of this portrait in these terms : " I have recently discovered, what was unknown to any one before, that the *second ring* on the index finger, left hand, has a crest or coat of arms on it—an exquisite miniature painting of two cocks fighting, then two scrolls ornamentally dividing it from something else beneath, that I am unable just at present to make out, because I cannot get near enough to it with a glass. I have the portrait and frame in a shadow box to protect it." (Cut No. 20.)

SECOND GROUP.

PICTURES, ENGRAVINGS, STATUES, AND BASS-RELIEFS, EXECUTED BY THE
ARTISTS IN STRICT ACCORDANCE WITH THE DESCRIPTIONS OF
THE ADMIRAL LEFT BY HIS CONTEMPORARIES.

To this group I will assign a few pictures and engravings. Statues and
bass-reliefs will be dealt with in their proper places in this work.

1. The Zschoch Engraving.
2. The Holt Engraving.
3. The Columbus of the Barabino Painting.
4. Wapper, Columbus in Chains.
5. The Riecke Engraving.
6. The Jacotin.
7. The Venetian Mosaic.

21—THE ZSCHOCH ENGRAVING.

THE ZSCHOCH ENGRAVING. — I
reproduce the Zschoch engraving,
which I believe is based on that
of Montanus, because it represents
Columbus with hair, mustache and
beard arranged somewhat after the
ancient Assyrian fashion, and were
it not for the ruff around the neck
he would resemble a pirate in a sensational drama. It has all the well-
known lineaments of Columbus, but
it is easily seen that it is an entirely
imaginary portrait. All that I know
about it is, that it is engraved by
Zschoch, and that I have three different copies of it, but I fail to find
the name of this engraver in any of
the biographical dictionaries I have
consulted. (Cut No. 21.)

THE HOLT ENGRAVING.—My object in presenting this picture to my readers is only to show how widely an entirely ideal portrait, possessing all the characteristics of Columbus, can differ from others having the same general features. It is the face of a man capable of realizing all the dreams of the Admiral. The execution is good, but, as a portrait of Columbus, it is entirely worthless. (Cut No. 22.)

THE NICOLO BARABINO PORTRAIT.—At the Orsini Palace in Genoa is one of the most powerful and beautiful paintings referring to the life of Columbus.

I regret that its very large size prevents me from presenting an engraving of it to my readers. I have taken the full length portrait of Columbus from it. (Cut No. 23.)

In the great and magnificently decorated hall of the convent of Santo Domingo, at Salamanca, many of its learned monks are assembled by order of the King and Queen. They have just listened to the demonstrations of Columbus, and nothing is more amusing than to see the different expressions on the faces of the good monks. Some look with wonder at

22—THE HOLT ENGRAVING.

the majestic man who is explaining to them doctrines entirely contrary to what their scientific lore has taught them; others cross their hands and bow their heads as if praying heaven to pardon the man who is expounding such impious ideas; others take things more easily, they simply believe the poor sailor is a *crank* of the harmless class, and laugh at him; one turns away his head, in order that he may laugh to his heart's content; another tries to conceal his grinning face with a book, while still another points his finger at his own forehead, and appears to be indicating to his brethren that "that fellow's mind is not well-balanced." One of the most magnificent faces is that of an old monk by the side of Columbus, leaning heavily against the wooden railing, and looking at the face of the Admiral with an expression of the most profound astonishment, wondering whether he be a genius or a fool.

But the figure of Columbus is something superb. Barabino has given him a cast of face tallying admirably with the descriptions we have of him. His high forehead, uncombed and flowing hair, eagle eyes, magnificent nose and energetic mouth, show how he is repressing his indignation at seeing that these men, who are to be the arbiters of the realization of his life plans, cannot understand him and are laughing in derision at what they in their ignorance, consider as the dreams of a fool.

23—COLUMBUS FROM THE N. BARABINO PICTURE.

THE WAPPERS PORTRAIT.—From a beautiful engraving in a French illustrated paper, I have taken the portrait of Columbus which appears in the
famous historical painting by Wappers, "Columbus in Chains." The artist

24—COLUMBUS IN WAPPERS' PORTRAIT.

has followed the descriptions of Columbus and idealized his face. I very much
regret that I cannot present the whole picture, but the only engraving I have
been able to find in the United States is copyrighted by the *Magazine of*

American History, and my request for permission to reproduce it has met with a peremptory refusal. (Cut No. 24.)

THE RIECKE PORTRAIT.—In the work by Dr. G. A. Riecke, entitled, *Christoph Columbus der Entdecker Amerika's*, there is a beautiful engraving representing Columbus in chains on board the ship which is carrying him home to Spain. The Admiral is shown reclining at the foot of a mast, the sea being represented in the background. He is clothed in black, with a large light-colored mantle partially enveloping him. He has long hair with a full beard and is leaning on his left hand, while with the right he is trying to lessen the weight of his heavy fetters. The expression of the face is admirable and accords with the descriptions of Columbus, but at the same time it does not resemble the generally accepted type.

JACOTIN.—Among the many so-called portraits of Columbus which I have in my collection, I have selected this one for publication only on account of its beauty. It has also many of the lineaments characteristic of Columbus, yet it is entirely ideal. I have copied it from a photograph given to me by Mr. Ernesto de Zaldo, of this city, who bought it in Paris, in the photographic gallery of Jacotin. It resembles none of the other portraits of Columbus which I have seen. (Cut No. 25.)

THE VENETIAN MOSAIC.— In 1867 the Common Council of the city of Venice resolved to send as a present to her ancient rival, Genoa, two beautiful mosaics of two great Genoese, Marco Polo and Christopher Columbus. This was an act of reciprocity, as Genoa had not long before presented Venice with the busts of Pietro D'Oria and Vettor Pisani.

The mosaic is a magnificent piece of work, six feet and a half high, beautifully framed in black marble. The figure of Columbus is depicted on a gold background, clothed in the dress of a Venetian nobleman of the fifteenth century. Columbus is clean shaved ; the hair is not very

25—THE JACOTIN PORTRAIT.

long ; he wears a barret cap and holds a map in his hand. He has a low-necked shirt with a ruff, and an ample mantle of velvet with silk lapels. The model followed appears to be that of the Jovian portrait. (Cut No. 26.)

26—THE VENETIAN MOSAIC.

THIRD GROUP.

IMAGINARY PORTRAITS AND ENGRAVINGS.

As it is utterly impossible to classify these portraits in any systematic order, according to generally recognized rules, I have therefore, arranged them in alphabetical sequence, so that any one desired may be readily found.

THE ALBANY PORTRAIT.—This picture bears the inscription ANNO 1492 ÆT. 23. It was probably painted by some Spanish artist in commemoration of the first anniversary of the discovery, and the age of the artist was twenty-three years. Mr. Curtis' supposition that it purports to represent Columbus at the age of twenty-three years is entirely untenable. A cursory inspection of the picture shows that Columbus is represented as a man of about fifty years. The picture itself is of very little value, but it is very old and it was presented to the State in 1784, by Mrs. Maria Farmer, a grandchild of Jacob Leisler, Governor of the Province of New York, in 1689. It is hung to-day in the Senate Chamber at Albany, and is considered the oldest picture of Columbus in the United States.

ARCHIVES OF THE INDIES.—This picture is a duplicate of the one in the Veragua Palace at Madrid, taken many years afterwards. It presents Columbus clad in armor as a young man with a pointed mustache; he also wears a ruff and slashed trowsers.

I remember having read in *Ford* that "this picture is quite as apocryphal, and by no means so beautiful as that of Parmigianino at Naples."

THE BERWICK-ALBA PORTRAIT.—In the gallery of the Duke of Berwick-Alba, in Madrid, is a magnificent painting representing Columbus. The dress shows that it is a work of the seventeenth century, and though it is very beautiful, is entirely untrustworthy. It is very large, and shows Columbus seated in a very rich chair of state. Carderera describes it thus: "He is clothed in a red tunic sprinkled with golden flowers, over which he wears a kind of ducal mantle richly embroidered with the same metal, with an ermine tippet on the shoulders. He holds a "carried" sword. I have never seen any copy of this picture just as it is. It was engraved by the famous artist, Rafael Esteva, in a vigorous and masterly manner, following the drawing made by the painter Galiano from the aforesaid picture. But there are some very curious points about this engraving; the first is, that the original is seated and holds a sword in his hand, while in the engraving he is shown standing with the sword sheathed and his hand on his hip, and there is some

change in the background. The second, that at the foot there is the following epigraph: "The original picture was painted in America, by Vanloo." No painter of that name was ever in America, nor was one of that name born within two centuries after the death of Columbus.

In this picture Columbus looks very young; he wears a mustache, with a small tuft of beard on the under lip; his hair is arranged in a very "dudish" fashion, and he wears the indispensable fluted ruff and ruffles.

Mr. Curtis says that there is a copy in oil of this portrait in the Lenox Library of New York, to which it was presented by Mr. James Lenox; but the only portrait existing in the Lenox

27—THE BERWICK-ALBA PORTRAIT, AS ENGRAVED.

Library is the one painted by Mr. Daniel Huntington in 1847. According to Mr. Huntington himself, from whom I have obtained this information, through the courtesy of Mr. Eames, the Assistant Librarian of the Lenox, "it is not a copy at all, but was based on a comparison of the engraved portraits, and therefore it really has no historical value." (Cut No. 27.)

THE JUAN DE BORGOÑA PORTRAIT.—The picture said to be in the Chapter Room of the Cathedral at Toledo, is supposed by some to have been painted by Juan de Borgoña, in 1519, thirteen years after the death of Columbus.

Curtis says that there is an engraving of it in one of the English editions of Irving, but I have been unable to find it.

I must state, however, that Pi y Margall, in his *History of Painting in Spain*, says "that such a picture does not exist there," and furthermore, "that there is not the slightest evidence that such a picture ever existed."

THE BOSSI MEDALLION.—In Bossi's *La Vera Patria e La Vita de Cristoforo Colombo*, there is a pretty little medallion representing Columbus. I believe it is taken from the De Bry medallion with some slight changes, as all the hard features are greatly softened. He also reproduces the large De Bry portrait. This medallion is entitled to no more credit than both the portraits of De Bry.

THE DE BRY PORTRAIT.—In the introduction to Part V. of the *Voyages*, which is the second part of the *Voyage of Benzoni*, there is a beautiful engraving, which many critics think is simply a copy with some variations of the Versailles portrait. It was first published in 1585, and has been reproduced in all the editions of *De Bry* and in many other works.

It represents Columbus with a broad heavy face, which is entirely Flemish in character, with a big, flat nose, and the hair arranged symmetrically in horizontal rows of curls, with a cap and the conventional dress. It will be seen immediately, that the features do not agree with the descriptions which we have of him.

De Bry claims that the original was painted from life by order of the Catholic Kings, before Columbus sailed on his first voyage of discovery, and that this original was stolen from the Hall of the Council of the Indies and taken to the Netherlands. He says also that as he had had the good fortune to obtain a copy of this portrait from a friend, who had received it from the artist himself, he desired to share his pleasure with his readers, and to this end, he caused it to be engraved on copper in a reduced form by his son.

Unluckily, all this is simply an advertisement to push the sale of his book, as the type of the face, the dress and style of this portrait, show that they are not of Spanish origin.

Mr. Rio says that it is not probable that in the camp before Granada or in the port of Palos, painters should be numerous, or that they should have any desire to portray Columbus, when nobody took the trouble to paint Boabdil, especially as the poor Genoese was considered to be somewhat of a visionary.

As the engraving is really a beautiful one and De Bry's works had a great reputation, it has been reproduced in a number of works, and it is to be regretted that even now it is presented as an authentic portrait of Columbus in some editions of *Washington Irving*, and in the last edition published in London of the *Historie* of Ferdinand Columbus.

This portrait is the one which represents Columbus with two warts upon the right cheek. Carderera says that these warts appeared only in the earliest prints, and that they were afterwards erased, but in my edition of *De Bry*, and in all those which I have seen, I have invariably found the warts. (Cut No. 28.)

QVI RATE VELIVOLA OCCIDVOS PENETRAVIT AD IDOS
PRIMVS ET AMERICAM NOBILITAVIT HVMVM

CHRISTOPHORVS COLVMBVS LIGVR INDIARV PRIM INVET A 1492

ASTRORVM CONSVLT, ET IPSO NOBILIS AVSV
CHRISTOPHOR TALI FRONTE COLVMBERAT

28—THE DE BRY ENGRAVING.

THE DE BRY VIGNETTE.—The medallion in *De Bry* (see cut No. 29), is truly beautiful from an artistic point of view, but is absolutely different in character from the large engraving by the same artist. This little picture

looks more like Columbus, and I believe the artist followed, to a certain
extent, the Capriolo or de Pas engravings.

A careful comparison with the little medallion
published by Bossi leads me to believe that the
Bossi portrait is taken from De Bry's, with some
alterations to make it appear an original engraving.
(Cut No. 29.)

29—THE DE BRY
MEDALLION.

THE CARTHAGENA PORTRAIT.—Mr. Jomard, in a
very able essay on the portraits of Columbus, enlarged
upon the great importance of the picture supposed to
exist in the Navy Yard, at Carthagena, Spain. On
petition of Mr. Carderera, the Spanish Government ordered it to be sent to
Madrid for examination. This order could not be complied with, as within
the memory of man no such picture had ever been in the Navy Yard;
and, furthermore, no mention could be found in any inventory of the Yard
that any such portrait had ever existed there, nor is any reference made to
it in any Spanish work.

THE CLADERA ENGRAVING.—This engraving is a half-length picture of
Columbus, as a young man with a mustache and goatee. He is clothed in full
armor, and wears a fluted ruff and wristbands, which were not worn until
half a century after his death. A silk sash passes over the right shoulder and
crosses the body. The right hand only is visible in the act of pointing to his
discoveries on a globe. This globe is held in the left hand. His finger
hinders a view of the West Indies, but in the portion of the globe which is
visible all the coast of America, from the Gulf of Mexico to Greenland, is
perfectly shown. The mouths of the St. Lawrence as well as Hudson's and
Baffin's Bays are plainly to be seen, which proves that the original from
which it was taken must have been posterior to the seventeenth century, or
that the artist who copied it was guilty of gross anachronisms.

Cladera says, page 32: "The portrait of Christopher Columbus has been
drawn from an original full-length painting about two yards long, which was
the property of his son Fernando, the character of which warrants us in the
belief that it was painted at the beginning of the sixteenth century. This
picture is in the house of José Colon, of His Majesty's Council, who gave
permission to copy it. It agrees whith the descriptions which Don Fernando
has given of the features of his father."

It was painted by Antonio Carnicero and engraved by Simon Brieva.
Carnicero was born in 1748. He studied at Rome, was painter to the King,
and died in 1814. The engraving is beautiful; but, notwithstanding what

Cladera says of the artistic merit of the original painting from which it was taken, it is absolutely worthless as a historical portrait.

There is a great similarity between this picture and the one in the house of

CHRISTOVAL COLON.
Descubridor de la America.

30—THE CLADERA PORTRAIT.

the Duke of Berwick-Alba, which I reproduce elsewhere. The original of this picture is, according to Mr. Curtis, in the gallery of the Duke of Veragua.

Mr. Curtis, by an oversight, says that it was engraved by Carnicero and that the signature is, Bart. Vasque La Grabó. I am sure that this has been

31—THE FLAMENG ETCHING.

caused by the carelessness of the amanuensis, as Mr. Curtis had my own copy of Cladera, which reads very clearly, "A. Carnicero del," "Simn. Brieva sculp." (See the Vasquez Portrait.) (Cut No. 30.)

COLUMBINA.—The portrait in this famous library, founded by Fernando Colon, the natural son of the Admiral, was presented to the library about half a century ago, by King Louis Philippe of France. The attitude is one of contemplation, and though it follows the description of Columbus, it is easy to see that it is a work of imagination. This, besides the evidence of its being modern, renders it of very small importance, whatever may be its artistic merit. The name of the artist who painted it is Mr. Charles Legros.

THE CONCORD PORTRAIT.—All I know about this portrait is what Mr. Curtis says respecting it in his article in *The Cosmopolitan Magazine*. He remarks that "an alleged portrait of Columbus hangs in the public library at Concord, Massachusetts, but it bears no resemblance to the traditional appearance of Columbus. It was presented to the library in 1873, by Mr. A. P. Chamberlaine, and is a copy by Raphael Mengs of an alleged Spanish portrait. It was formerly in the collection of Letizia Bonaparte, Napoleon's mother—'Madame Mère'—at Rome, and was purchased by Mr. Chamberlaine after her death. There is a legend that Mengs, the artist, left a record somewhere that he made a copy of a portrait of Columbus by Titian, but this record cannot now be found, nor is there any evidence that Titian and Columbus ever met."

BOL OR ERMITAGE.—Among the superb works of art which make up this magnificent gallery, founded by Catherine of Russia, and now the property of the Czars, this pretended portrait of Columbus, painted by Ferdinand Bol, a Flemish artist born in 1610, and who died in 1681, occupies a very conspicuous position. He was the best disciple of Rembrandt, whom he copied so faithfully that many of his works have been attributed to the hand of the Master. I regret to say that in the catalogue of the Ermitage Gallery I have not been able to find a description of such an important picture. Mention only is made among the other works of Bol, of a *"Portrait of a man with a black hat."* Can this be the pretended Columbus?

THE LEOPOLD FLAMENG PORTRAIT.—In *The Life of Columbus* by the Marquis du Belloy (Paris), there is a splendid etching by the famous artist Leopold Flameng, assuming to represent Christopher Columbus. The book also includes many other superb etchings of incidents in the life of the Admiral. Unhappily, their artistic merit is in inverse ratio to their historical worth. It seems incredible that so talented an artist as Flameng should not have been more accurate in portraying the types and dress, as well as the accessories of the period, his celebrated etchings not having the slightest resemblance to any thing Spanish.

A mere glance at the masterly etching (No. 31) will show that this tall, commanding man with the plumed cap, cuirass and cloak with loose sleeves, and with his hand on the hilt of his sword, may be some condottiere of the sixteenth or seventeenth centuries, but could not possibly be Christopher Columbus. Yet the picture is so beautiful, and the book has been translated into so many languages, generally accompanied by these illustrations, that i must yield to the temptation of presenting it to my readers. (Cut No. 31.)

FONTAINE.— Danlos published this portrait, which has been painted by Fontaine, and engraved by Pedro Colón, Duke of Veragua. I do not agree with Mr. Curtis, who believes it is a copy of the portrait in the Naval Museum, with a more cheerful expression. I believe it is a copy from the portrait in the house of the Duke of Veragua.

THE LUCCA GIORDANO POR-TRAIT.— There is in a palace at Genoa a beautiful picture of Columbus by Lucca "Fa Presto." It represents Columbus as almost a boy with curly hair, attired in the garb of a Franciscan, with a chain around the neck and holding a quadrant in the right hand. The lineaments do not correspond in any respect to those of the Admiral; and, although the painting is charming, it has not the least value as a portrait. (Cut No. 32.)

I will say that, as compared with the Edwards' picture, which, as I say elsewhere, is the ugliest portrait of the Admiral I have seen, this is the one in which he looks the handsomest. (Cut No. 32.)

32—THE LUCCA GIORDANO PORTRAIT.

THE HAVANA PORTRAIT.—This picture was presented in 1796 (and not two hundred years ago, as Mr. Curtis says), by the Duke of Veragua to the municipality of Havana, as a token of gratitude for the honors rendered by the people of Havana to the supposed remains of his ancestor, Christopher Columbus, on their arrival in that city during the preceding year.

I have often seen it. It is a most miserable daub, and is in very bad condition. No one can believe that it is intended to be a portrait of Columbus. He is represented as clothed in the garb of a familiar of the Inquisition—has long flowing hair, pointed mustache and very small goatee, with black eyes and protruding underlip; he also wears a ridiculous big white collar and cuffs. He holds in the left hand a globe. The inscription, "*Por Castilla y por Leon Nuevo Mundo ayo Colon*," is in one of the corners. Some people believe it to be the picture of the natural son of the Admiral, Don Fernando, who was a churchman. It bears not the slightest resemblance to any other old picture of Columbus.

The painting was originally 80 by 60 centimètres in size.

Happily for his posthumous reputation, the name of the painter of this daub is absolutely unknown. (Cut No. 33.)

THE HERRERA PORTRAIT.—This is taken from the French edition of *Herrera*, and has been reproduced in Bryant & Gay's *History of the United States*. I believe it is taken from the Montanus portrait. It was also engraved in the English edition of *Herrera*, translated by John Stevens and published in London, in 6 vols., 1725-1726, under the name of *A General History of America*. As a portrait, it is absolutely worthless, but it has been reproduced in many other works.

33—THE HAVANA PORTRAIT.

HERRERA, (VIGNETTE).—This portrait was published in the edition of *Herrera*, dated 1601, and looks very much like the *De Bry* vignette, and probably they are of the same origin.

This vignette was reproduced in the edition of *Barcia* (1726-1730), but I do not agree with Winsor when he states that the one in Bryant & Gay is a reproduction of this vignette.

HULL.—I am indebted to the kindness of Mr. Curtis for a copy of this beautiful portrait, and as all I know regarding it is what Mr. Curtis states in his able articles in *The Cosmopolitan*, I will therefore transcribe the paragraphs relating to it verbatim :

"Miss Esther Hull, of Danbury, Connecticut, has a portrait of Columbus which is of evident antiquity, but there is no knowledge of its age or origin. It represents Columbus of middle age, with a dove resting upon his shoulder, and there is a companion piece of Amerigo Vespucci by the same artist. All

the owner knows of their history is that many years ago they were left for storage with Mr. William Jaggers of New York, with several other paintings. In 1850, the owner wrote Mr. Jaggers from a western State that he had met with reverses and desired to sell his collection. The two portraits were purchased by the father of Miss Hull, who brought them to Danbury. At the left hand upper corner of each canvas is an inscription. On one is, 'Amerigo Vespucci;' on the other 'Cristoforo Colombo,' which indicates that the artist was an Italian."

34.—THE HERRERA PORTRAIT.

THE HUNTINGTON PORTRAIT.—The portrait in the Lenox Gallery, New York, is one of the best works from the brush of the distinguished artist, David Huntington. It represents the Admiral in a three-quarter length, with a full beard and wearing a cap, and a fur-trimmed mantle. In one hand he holds a scroll, while the other rests on a small globe placed on a table. Notwithstanding its artistic merit, Mr. Huntington himself has stated that the picture is one compiled from a comparison of different engravings, and it has therefore no historical value. (See Berwick-Alba portrait.)

35—THE HERRERA WOODCUT.

JOMARD. — This superb picture, discovered by Jomard in the gallery at Vicenzo, in Italy, in 1844, is supposed by some critics to be the work of Titian, or of one of his disciples, Domenico Campagnola, but there is no proof that Titian or Campagnola ever met Columbus; and furthermore the picture shows by its details that it was painted many years after the death of the Admiral. I copy from Mr. Curtis' interesting article what Jomard says about it: "The Jomard portrait is so called in honor of a distinguished scholar and critic,

Mr. Jomard, for many years librarian of the Bibliothèque Nationale, Paris, who discovered it in a gallery at Vicenza, Italy, in 1844. 'I saw it by chance,' says Mr. Jomard (*in Bulletin de la Société de Géographie Troisième Série, Tome III.*, 1843), 'though I was attracted by the ancient appearance of the painting, by its beauty, and by the noble character of the

36—THE HULL PORTRAIT.

whole figure. Drawing nearer to the painting, what was my surprise when I saw in old gold letters of the style of the time, on the right angle, these two words: Christoforus Columbus. It will easily be believed that I lost no time in collecting all information apt to enlighten me as to its origin.

Thanks to the kindness of the noble and learned Count Orti Manava, Podestà of Verona, I was soon in possession of all facts. It will be easily understood

37—THE JOMARD PORTRAIT.

why such a treasure remained so long unknown. The family owning it kept it carefully, although unaware of its importance. The last member bequeathed it to his native city and at his death it was placed in the public gallery."

Carderera believes that this picture, whoever the artist may be, was painted at the beginning of the seventeenth century, about the time of Philip III, as the dress is in exact accordance with the costume of that period, and that the name on it, Christophorus Columbus, was added at a later date, and is simply an imposture.

Jomard claims that this picture embodies all the characteristics of Columbus, and that the anachronisms are the work of later times; but this is carrying his contention to the verge of absurdity.

Though this picture has been reproduced in many modern works, I do not think that any one to-day considers it as authentic. (Cut No. 37.)

JULIUS ROMANUS.—In the Municipal Palace at Genoa there is a large picture containing two medallions, one representing Columbus and the other

38—THE JULIO ROMANO PORTRAIT.

Americus Vespucius: the artist was undoubtedly a great master, and by common consent, this picture has been attributed to Julio Romano, who died in 1546. It looks somewhat like the Crispin de Pas cut and may be a copy of some sketch made in Spain: yet I fail to find in it the well-known features of the Discoverer. (Cut No. 38.)

THE MENGS PORTRAIT.—I have sometimes read that Raphael Mengs painted a portrait of Columbus in the last century, which was copied from an old master and some even say that this old master was Titian. I have carefully examined the catalogue of the works of Mengs, as well as many biographies of this famous artist, but have failed to find reference to any such portrait. The Concord portrait, already mentioned, has been supposed to be this much sought-for painting, but so far as I can gather this picture cannot possibly be the work of such a master as Mengs.

MONTANUS.—Opposite page 44, of my copy of *Dr. O. Dapper, Die Unbekante Neue Welt*, Amsterdam, 1673, there is a splendid copper plate engraving purporting to represent Columbus. It is supposed to be a copy from a picture painted at Nuremberg, in 1661. It first appeared in the Dutch edition of *Montanus* in 1671: then in *Dapper*, who pirated it from Montanus, and also in *Ogilby's America*. I believe Mr. Curtis is perfectly right in considering the portrait published in Herrera and adopted by Bryant as a copy of the Montanus engraving, with some slight changes. (Cut No. 39.)

THE MUÑOZ PORTRAIT.—The frontispiece of the *Historia del Nuevo Mundo*, is a copy from the original of Mariano Maella and was not painted one

39—THE MONTANUS ENGRAVING.

hundred years after the death of Columbus, as Mr. Curtis erroneously says. Maella died in 1819, and was the General Director of the Academy of San

Fernando, and Court Painter to the King up to the time of his death. Maella followed the painting in the gallery of Veragua or that in the Archives of the Indies, reproducing it with the cuirass and ruff. This portrait is very similar to that of Cladera, even in the wearing of the sash across the breast. It has a

40—THE MUÑOZ PORTRAIT.

heavy mustache and a small, full, closely clipped beard. It has been reproduced a number of times, with changes dictated more or less by the fancy of the artist. According to Carderera, it is not deserving of much credit. I have about one dozen copies of it and they all differ, more or less.

Mr. Curtis says that a copy of this picture was presented in 1818, by R. W. Mead to the Pennsylvania Academy of Arts, but it has disappeared. (Cut No. 40.)

THE PARMIGIANINO PORTRAIT.—Perhaps the most beautiful of all the pretended portraits of the Admiral now in existence, is the one at Naples, in the Real Museo Borbonico, which is the work of the chaste and correct brush of Francesco Mazzuola, better known as "il Parmigianino."

This superb panel has challenged the admiration of all who have seen it, on account of its beauty, and has been reproduced everywhere. Unhappily, it is a purely imaginative work, and as Becchi justly says, in his famous work on the Real Museo Borbonico, is not deserving of the slightest confidence.

Carderera, who has examined it carefully, does not believe that the artist ever intended it to represent Columbus. Not even the slightest point of resemblance is to be found between the descriptions of the Admiral and the face in this painting. It represents a courtier of insinuating manners and forbidding appearance. The difference is still greater between the dress and austere aspect of Columbus and the elaborate and effeminate ornaments of this personage, whose head also is entirely different in shape from that of the Admiral. The hair is arranged in elegant and symmetrical curls, which, as well as the long beard, are most carefully combed and crimped, a thing very rarely seen in the time of Ferdinand and Isabella in Italy and Spain. Still more out of fashion is the red cap, slashed after the Dutch mode, and with feathers and gilt button. The same thing can be said of all the rest of his attire and even of the ring which he wears.

Carderera says that one of the causes which has given rise to the pretension that this picture represents Columbus is the clasp on the cap, on which is the representation of a ship passing beyond the Pillars of Hercules. Even in case this is true, it may be simply one of the devices commonly used by notable persons of the time, for whom Jovius, Ruscelli, Capaccio and other famous Italians published their costly works. Don Garcia de Toledo, who was Viceroy of Catalonia, used a compass as his device: Isabel de Cocceggio, displayed two anchors in the sea: Estevan Colonna, two columns on the high sea with a ribbon uniting them, a siren between them and the motto, "*His saffulla*," and none of them were discoverers. This picture bearing the name of Christopher Columbus, was for many years in the Farnese Gallery and has been described by many distinguished writers, who have overlooked all the inconsistencies in it. It has also been reproduced in many works: even Prescott in his *History of the Catholic Kings*, has adopted it, but at present nobody considers it to be a portrait of Columbus, and some believe that it is a

portrait of Gilberto de Sassuoli, a distinguished nobleman who was born in
1502 and died in 1570.

That the picture could never have been taken from life is very easily

41—THE PARMIGIANINO PORTRAIT.

established by stating the fact that Mazzuola was born in 1503 and died in
1540, and was therefore, only three years of age at the time of the death of
Columbus. He was a disciple of Raphael and painted many beautiful

portraits, among them one of Americus Vespucius. The pretended portrait of Columbus was painted at Parma, in 1527, by order of Cardinal Alessandro Farnesi. The King of Naples was his heir and removed it to Naples. I have

Almirante de navies para las Indias.

42—THE PHILOPONUS ENGRAVING.

also seen a beautiful copy of this portrait on a bank note of the Republic of Santo Domingo, and I have been told by a friend that he has seen it on bills issued by some State banks in this country. The engraving by Bierstadt on certain United States bank notes appears to be a copy of the same picture with some very noticeable changes. (Cut No. 41.)

THE PHILOPONUS PORTRAIT.—The first plate in the curious work of Honorius Philoponus, *Nova Typis Transacta Navigatio*, &c., &c., printed in 1621, but with no mention of the place of publication, is a full length portrait of Columbus. As I reproduce it, and it has no particular history or historical value, I do not consider it necessary to give any description of it, but will merely call the attention of my readers to the extraordinary dress and cap worn by the Admiral, as well as to the very original map in which the name of America is given only to the northern part of the United States. I would also like to call attention to the quaint inscriptions on the said map and the design of the caravel. (Cut No. 42.)

SEBASTIAN DEL PIOMBO.—Among the treasures in the Bibliothèque Nationale of Paris, is a beautiful wood engraving which bears the following inscription :

HÆC EST EFFIGIES LIGURI MIRANDI COLUMBI
ANTIPODUM PRIMUS RATE QUI PENETRAVIT IN ORBEM.
and signed.

SEBASTIANUS VENETUS FECIT.

which means :

"This is the portrait of the wonderful Genoese Columbus, the first who in a ship reached the world of the antipodes :

Sebastian the Venetian made it."

I have never seen a copy of it nor even a description, but M. R. Darzens, writing of it in the Paris *Figaro*, says: "Notwithstanding the inscription, it does not bear the least resemblance to the de Orchi portrait, which is claimed to be the original Jovius portrait." He proceeds to remark humorously : "There are in addition—in the Bibliothèque Nationale, where I have unearthed forty-six different types, of a more or less recent date, reproducing the features of Christopher Columbus,—a number of old engravings. There is something there to suit all tastes. There are fat Columbuses, thin, bearded, mustached, long-haired, bald, in fact as I have said, something to suit all tastes, which excuses me from discussing them."

RIBERA.—The figure of Columbus in the large fresco in the Hall of Sessions of the Palace of Deputies at Madrid, is the work of Carlos Luis de Ribera, but although it is of great artistic merit it has no pretensions to be considered a portrait of Columbus.

THE RINCK PORTRAIT.—Some days after the close of the sessions of the Congress of Americanists, held at Luxemburg, in 1877, a letter was forwarded to the Committee on Publication by Baron de Dumast, who had received it from Mr. Rinck, a French portrait painter of New York. The letter was accompanied by a picture which under any circumstances deserves to be reproduced, if only for the amusement of my readers.

I will not follow Mr. Rinck in his original argument in favor of the authenticity of this picture, for I cannot believe for a moment that so talented an artist as he is, would seriously maintain that the old miser weighing an egg in his emaciated hand, is intended to represent Columbus, and that the grotesque lineaments of so vulgar a face, agree with the well-known noble and energetic features of the Admiral, and at the same time I cannot consider it as a practical joke perpetrated on Baron Dumast.

Mr. Rinck says that in 1845 or 1846, being in New Orleans, he attended an auction sale where he saw the picture which was catalogued under the title,

43—THE RINCK PORTRAIT.

Le Vieux Gastronome, and that recognizing at a glance, the merit of the picture he bid for and secured it, amid the sneers of the bystanders! I think the bystanders were perfectly right, as the subject of the miserable daub seems to be joining in the sneers at the absurd claim made in its favor. The poor old man is attired in a semi-military old coat, of brown and red—the Spanish colors, as Rinck says—being, as is well-known, red and yellow. The coat belongs to the Eighteenth if not to the Nineteenth century.

The joke, however, has been carried too far, and it is not my intention to contribute to such an exibition of bad taste. (Cat No. 43.)

SCARDONI.—The Worcester Antiquarian Society possesses a picture of Columbus painted by Scardoni. I have been told that it resembles the Moro portrait but have been unable to find a description of it.

SCOTTO.—The portrait engraved by Scotto, copied from a design by Belloni, is nothing more than the De Bry picture, with the addition of a small mustache, which makes it still more ridiculous than the original.

THÉVET, (First Picture).—There are two portraits of Columbus published by Thévet ; one of them is described by Curtis, and is reproduced in Cut No. 44.

Mr. Curtis says in his article in the *Cosmopolitan*, regarding this picture :
" André Thévet, in his *Portraits et Vies des Hommes Illustres* which was first
published in Paris in 1584, gives us a Columbus of a solemn type that looks
more like an astrologer of the middle ages than a seaman.   It is a rude woodcut and has been frequently copied.   It appears in N. D. Clerck's *Tooneel der*

44—THE THÉVET CUT.

Beroemder Hertogen, published at Delft in 1617; in North's edition of *Plu-
tarch's Lives*, published at Cambridge in 1676; Isaac Bullart's *Académie
des Sciences et des Arts*, published at Brussels in 1682, and in several other
works of later date.   Clerck says that Thévet obtained the portrait in Lisbon,
and that it was painted by a Dutch artist while Columbus was living there."

I may add that though the engraving is very rough, it is splendidly designed; and the face is that of a man of extraordinary intelligence and energy, and though not resembling in the least the Jovian type, yet it agrees fully with the descriptions we have of Columbus.

The five large stars in the background are, according to the opinions of

45—THE THÉVET ENGRAVING.

some, the great Southern constellation, the "Cross," which can be seen during part of the year from almost any place in the regions discovered by Columbus; others believe it to be the "Great Bear."

The second Thévet portrait is a very good engraving from a copper-plate. The face is full of intelligence and energy, but the eyebrows, the eyes, the forehead, the nose and the mouth are entirely different from those of the other portrait : there is not the least resemblance between them.

Thevet's works have enjoyed great popularity. They are at present rare ; but as a curiosity, there is quite a demand for them. I do not think that among the portraits with which his works are illustrated, there is a single one deserving of any confidence ; the engraving No. 45 is taken from one of the German editions of his works.

THE VASQUEZ PORTRAIT.—The origin of the Cladera, Muñoz and Vasquez pictures, and of the high-relief in the Cathedral at Havana, is very curious. About the end of the last century, the Duke of Veragua found among the collection of pictures belonging to the family, a beautiful painting of a man seated on a sort of a throne, attired as a grandee of Spain, bearing the inscription of *D. Cristobal Colon*. Believing it to be the picture of the great Admiral, he at once instructed the celebrated engraver Vasquez to make a copper-plate of it, stating that the original was in the gallery of the family. As the Vasquez engraving was a magnificent work of art and the engraver had the high authority of a descendant of Columbus as to its authenticity, no doubt was entertained as to the correctness of the claim. Muñoz accepted the picture as did Cladera, and when the high-relief was ordered for the Cathedral at Havana, this engraving was the original from which it was taken, no attention being paid to the anachronisms in the dress and the type of the picture, which cannot possibly be a portrait of Columbus if we consult the pen portraits of him left by his contemporaries.

This engraving has been widely copied : the more especially because it had been accepted by such eminent authorities as Muñoz and Cladera. The beautiful original of this engraving was never intended as a portrait of the Admiral, but of his grandson, Cristobal Colon y Toledo, brother of the third Admiral of the Indies, D. Luis, the son of D. Diego, son of the Discoverer. The age, type, and accessories of the picture described on page 69, which is still in the Veragua gallery, agree exactly with the appearance of the person whom it is now known to represent.

The engraving is of large size and bears the inscription:—*"CHRISTOVAL COLON—COPIADO DE UN QUADRO ORIGL., QUE SE CONSERVA EN LA FAMILIA—BART VAZQUE LA GRABO* 1791." It is a three-quarter-length portrait of Columbus, in which he is represented as a young man clad in armor with a ruff around the neck. He wears a mustache and goatee and holds a globe in his right hand and in the left a baton of command.

THE VERAGUA PORTRAIT.—The portrait in the gallery of the Duke of

Veragua, one of the descendants of the Admiral, was painted at the end of the XVIth century. It retains some of the features of the Columbus face, but he is represented as a young man with mustache and goatee, wearing a ruff and cuffs, which were worn at the time it was painted; Carderera considers it to be worthless. It is claimed that this portrait is a copy from an original which was carried from Santo Domingo to Havana, together with the supposed remains of Columbus, at the close of the last century. Such an original was not received at Havana, and probably never existed in Santo Domingo. The only portrait at Havana is one sent, in 1796, by the Duke of Veragua, the great-grandfather of the present Duke. It is, perhaps, a portrait of Don Fernando Colon, the son of the Admiral. It is said that this original picture was painted on board, and was about 18 or 20 inches in height; no one, to my knowledge, has ever seen it.

THE VERSAILLES PORTRAIT, No. 1.—In the Versailles Gallery there is a beautiful portrait painted on wood, which was presented to the Gallery long ago, by the Count de Montesquieu. Though it has great artistic merit, it is absolutely worthless as a portrait, as it has none of the characteristics of Columbus. It is a bust; the face is very broad and clean-shaven, with a big flat nose, large dark eyes, and long hair almost concealed by a cap. According to Carderera, the dress and cap are an exact reproduction of the fashion of the time of the Catholic Kings; yet Feuillet des Conches calls them strange and exotic.

Feuillet des Conches believes that it was painted by a disciple of John de Bruges or Van Eyck, as both the type and the style are Flemish; others say that it may have been painted at Lisbon, while Columbus was at that Court.

It is undoubtedly very old and bears so close a resemblance to the de Bry portrait, that it is believed to be the original followed by that artist; yet the de Bry has two well-defined warts on the right cheek and the Versailles has none.

This portrait has been engraved very often and the best representation of it is the beautiful plate by Mercuri. It has also been reproduced by Gavard in the *Galerie Historique de Versailles* and Mr. Curtis mentions thirteen copies of it including the de Bry in 1595. It is catalogued at the Museum as a work of the XVIth century under No. 2,997. (Cut No. 46.)

THE VERSAILLES PORTRAIT, No. 2.—The best notice I have found of the second portrait at Versailles, is that written by Mr. Curtis, and, as this gentleman has kindly authorized me to make any use I desire of his essay and cuts, I copy verbatim from his often quoted article in *The Cosmopolitan*. Mr. Curtis says: "The second Versailles portrait which is said to have disappeared

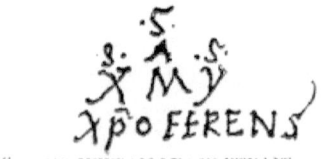

46   THE VERSAILLES PORTRAIT.

during the Franco-Prussian war, was very ancient also, and plainly of Dutch origin. It was painted on a small panel of wood twelve by fourteen centimètres in size. There was an anchor on the frame and on the right side of the figure an inscription of eight lines in ancient Dutch, which reads : 'Cristoff de Colomb, Groots Admiral Vost Zee onder Ferrand,' that is, 'Christopher Columbus, Grand Admiral of the Eastern Seas under Ferainand.' The head was completely bald, and the costume a great coat, or vitchouva, worn by sailors in the beginning of the sixteenth century. Its antiquity was evident, not only in the materials used, but because the costume, the style of letters and orthography of the inscription were not in vogue later than 1650."

ANONYMOUS.—In the *Illustrated American Biography*, published at New York, in 1853, by Jones and Emerson, there is a beautiful wood engraving which it is pretended is a half-length portrait of Columbus, omitting the hands. The

47—ANONYMOUS CUT.

face is noble and commanding and the eyebrows strictly historical ; the forehead is high and intellectual, but the nose, mouth and eyes have not the well-known characteristics of Columbus. The hair is quite long and he wears a full beard and mustache ; he is clad in armor, with the right shoulder half covered by a mantle. It has been copied in many American educational works, and that is the reason for my describing it ; as a portrait it is absolutely worthless.

ANONYMOUS.—The allegorical picture of Columbus which I reproduce in cut No. 47 has been published in many geographical works. It looks like a reproduction of the Parmigianino portrait, and is therefore worth no more than the original from which it was taken. On the one side the crews of Columbus are seen disembarking from his ships on an island covered with palms, and on the other is a thriving manufacturing town. Unluckily the

sword traversing the background of the picture, also shows allegorically the
instrument by which the conquest was accomplished.

COLUMBUS ON HORSEBACK.—GENOA.—In the Paradiso di Albaro, belonging

48—BRYAN-EDWARDS COLUMBUS AND HIS FAMILY.

to the Saluzzo family, there is a large portrait of Columbus on horseback,
riding over one of the islands he has discovered. We are told that the picture
is very beautiful and full of life and light, that the luxuriant vegetation of the

tropics is shown to advantage and with truth, but as the head is purely imaginary, it has no value as a portrait.

The Bryan-Edwards Picture.—I think it is proper to conclude this long enumeration of the portraits of Columbus, by a family group representing the Admiral, Beatriz, Don Diego and Don Fernando. This engraving is in the fourth edition of the *History of the West Indies*, published in London, in 1807, and it is copied " from an ancient Spanish picture in the possession of Edward Horne, Esq., of Bevis Mount, near Southampton," so says Edwards.

Edwards also claims that the date of the picture is about 1504, at the time of the return of Columbus from his fourth voyage, and the evidence that he adduces to this effect, incidentally establishes the fact that it is apocryphal.

He says that the Mar del Sud is marked on the original map, and as the Southern Sea was not discovered until 1513, by Balboa, it is absolutely impossible that this portrait could have been taken from life.

The portraits of Beatriz, Fernando and Diego, would be a great acquisition for the lovers of art from a historical point of view, but unfortunately this is a fact too good to be true : a mere glance is sufficient to convince us of the fallacy of the pretension, as the types, the dress, accessories and other particulars, show that this picture must have been painted at least one hundred years subsequent to the date claimed, and that the modest artist who painted it, and forgot to sign his name, had no intention of portraying so illustrious a family, but probably some rich Dutch merchant or planter, and his sons, who, after a lesson in geography, are preparing to partake of the luscious fruit, which a female servant wearing an *apron* is bringing to the table. A nondescript animal intended for a dog, but resembling a cross between a sheep and the former animal, is depicted as hungrily eying the head of the family.

The features of the servant and the boys are of the true Dutch type. In regard to Columbus, I will only say that this is the ugliest alleged portrait of him I have ever seen. (Cut No. 48.)

To this cursory and yet somewhat lengthy review of some of the so-called portraits of Columbus, I will add that there is in existence a very large number of paintings, engravings, lithographs, etc., purporting to represent Columbus, some of which are remarkable for their beauty, but not for their fidelity as most of them are imaginary pictures : among them I will mention the engravings by Landon, Fernando Selma (after Maella), Terla, Larmesin, Zatta, Bazin, etc., etc.

I will not attempt to give a catalogue of them, as this would fill a volume three or four times the size of the present, and they are not deserving of it, being in general only variations from the types already described.

Harrisse, Christopher Columbus and the Bank of St. George, p. 108, says:—"and we would then possess an authentic portrait of the discoverer of America, which does not exist anywhere, nor do I believe that the portrait of Columbus was ever painted, drawn or carved from the life." He further says that portrait painting commenced in Spain, at a later period than that of the Catholic Kings: this is an error as there are in existence portraits of the Catholic Kings, of the Princes, of Nebrija and of other persons painted by Rincon, who died in 1500.

Besides Rincon, the following artists of the same period have painted portraits: Juan Nuñez, Pedro de Cordova, Juan de Borgoña, Pedro Berruguete, Iñigo de Comontes, Alonso Sanchez, Luis de Medina, and N. Gallegos, and before the time of the Catholic Kings some portraits were also painted by Jorge Ingles and Juan Sanchez de Castro.

STATUES, MONUMENTS, BASS-RELIEFS, &c.,

IN MEMORY

OF COLUMBUS.

I WILL now proceed to describe the different monuments, statues bass-reliefs, &c., erected in honor of the great navigator, commencing with those in his native land and other parts of Europe. I will then follow him on his voyages, and afterwards describe the memorials in countries which he never visited, concluding with the United States.

ITALY.

MONUMENT AT GENOA.—In 1846, some citizens of Genoa organized a society for the purpose of raising a noble monument to the memory of their greatest fellow-citizen. The idea was approved by King Carlo Alberto, and in the same year, the Mayor of the city, Marquis Tommasso Spinola laid the corner-stone of the monument in the presence of a large number of distinguished Italians, at the Piazza dell' Acquaverde.

Some of the most eminent Italian sculptors submitted plans for the monument, and the Academy of Milan selected that of the great master Lorenzo Bartolini, who unfortunately died some months after. Then another eminent artist, Pietro Fraccia was chosen to carry into execution the plans of Bartolini, but he also, died in the same year.

The political disturbances of the following years, caused an almost complete cessation of the work ; the promised aid from the State and Municipality

49—THE MONUMENT AT GENOA.

could not be given in consequence of the demands incident to the war for Italian independence, and for the same cause the popular subscription was almost a complete failure. Another reason was the necessity of changing the site originally chosen for the monument to another place in the same Square, as a very large railroad depot had been built in the immediate vicinity. At last, thanks to the energetic efforts of the committee presided over by the Marquis Lorenzo Pareto, the monument was completed and dedicated on November 9th, 1862.

As this is up to the present time, one of the noblest monuments erected to the memory of the great Admiral, I consider it proper to give a detailed description of it to my readers. (Cut No. 49.)

The monument stands in the Piazza dell' Acquaverde; the base is a square of 40 feet on each side, stands on three steps, and has on each side, a bronze inscription in Italian; on the front it reads: "TO CHRISTOPHER COLUMBUS, THE FATHERLAND," on the right is, "FOUNDATION LAID IN 1846," and on the back are the words, "HAVING DIVINED A WORLD, HE FOUND IT FOR THE PERENNIAL BENEFIT OF THE OLD ONE;" "(divinato un mondo, lo accinse di perenni benefizi all' antico—1862)." On the left is, "THIS MONUMENT WAS DEDICATED IN 1862."

Three steps from the top of the base and in the center of it rises a highly ornamented cylindrical shaft, on the lower part of which are four bass-reliefs representing the most important events of the life of Columbus:

1. Columbus before the Council of Salamanca ;
2. Columbus erecting a cross on the first land discovered ;
3. Reception of Columbus at Barcelona, by the Kings of Spain on his return from the first voyage ;
4. Columbus in chains, returning to Spain.

The central part of the shaft is ornamented with beaks of ancient galleys, and on the top is a colossal statue of Columbus discovering America. At the suggestion of the Spanish government the lineaments of Columbus in the statue were taken from the portraits of Jovius and Capriolo. He has long, flowing hair, appears to be about fifty years of age and is dressed in scrupulous accordance with the fashion of the times, in a short Spanish tabard, and a large open cloak ; his left hand rests on an anchor while his right is on the shoulder of a figure of America typified by a kneeling Indian maiden holding a cross in the right hand.

At each of the four corners of the base, stands a smaller square pedestal, on each of which is a seated statue ; they represent Piety, Science, Constancy and Prudence.

The whole of the work in the monument is of great merit, but hardly any

50—CUSTODIA AT GENOA.

portion of it is the work of the artist to whom it was originally assigned. The grand group of Columbus and America, was designed and commenced by Bartolini ; after his death Fraccia continued it ; he also died and it was finished by the eminent sculptor, Franzini of Carrara. In consequence of the death of the principal artists, great changes were made in the staff. Certoli made the statue of Prudence and the bass-reliefs representing Columbus erecting the cross ; Vanni the statue of Piety ; and the bass-relief of the Reception at Barcelona was executed by Cevasco ; the bass-relief of the Council of Salamanca and the statue of Science, were the work of Gaggini, while Revelli, (the artist of the monument at Lima), made the bass-relief of Columbus in chains, and Santorelli the statue of Constancy ; the eight faces which ornament the lower base came from the studio of Rocchi in Carrara after models furnished by Vanni.

THE CUSTODIA OF GENOA.—Columbus presented Nicolo Oderigo with two complete sets of authenticated copies of his titles, to be placed for safe-keeping by him in the Bank of Genoa. These documents, together with three autograph letters of Columbus, were presented to the city of Genoa, by Laurentio Oderigo, a descendant of Nicolo Oderigo, and were accepted by a decree, dated January 10th, 1670. They were stolen during the political troubles of 1797, one passing into the possession of Count Cambiaso, the other being taken to Paris. The Government of Genoa secured the return of the papers, and after their recovery they were deposited in the archives of Genoa.

The Common Council ordered the erection of a "Custodia" for the purpose of the safety of these priceless documents, and Carlo Barabino, the City Architect, was entrusted with the execution of the work. The "Custodia" consists of a truncated column, in the upper part of which is a receptacle, closed by a metallic plate in which are deposited the precious relics, which are seldom exhibited to the public, and photographs of which are on view. The column is surmounted by a bust of Columbus ; it is about eight feet in height and stands on a square die. It bears the following inscription :

"QUÆ. HEIC. SUNT. MEMBRANAS. EPISTOLAS. Q. EXPENDITO. HIS. PATRIAM. IPSE. NEMPE. SUAM. COLUMBUS. APERIT. EN. QUID. MICHI. CREDITUM. THESAURI. SIET. DECR. DECURIONUM. GENUENS. M.DCCCXXI."

The bust is the work of the sculptor Peschiera ; it is four feet in height and is remarkable as a work of art, the artist having followed the descriptions of the Admiral, with the exception of the mouth and eyebrows, which are somewhat different. (Cut No. 50.)

THE GENOA STATUE.—At No. 19 Via Carlo Alberto, near the Piazze

Darsena, Genoa, Italy, a small statue of Columbus stands in a niche, with the following inscription :

" DISSI, VOLLI, CREDI, ECCO UN SECONDO
SORGER NUOVO, DALL' ONDE IGNOTO MONDO."

The statue is old and the artist's name unknown, but I have read that the artistic treatment is good, although it has no historic value. In addition to

51—BUST AT PAVIA.

this there are also in Genoa, two large busts, one at the University, and another at the Royal Palace. They both possess great artistic merit, but neither of them has any particular history.

Another statue of Columbus has been erected in the Red Palace at Genoa, which represents him standing on the deck of the Santa Maria behind a priest bearing a cross. The pedestal is ornamented by prows of caravels, and on each side are emblematic figures representing Discovery and Industry.

THE GENIUS OF COLUMBUS.—STATUE BY VIGNOLO.—This splendid work, which is of heroic size, is one of the most beautiful ornaments of the Royal Palace at Genoa.

STATUE IN THE GALLERY VITTORIO EMANUELE, MILAN.—There are in the Gallery Vittorio Emanuele, Milan, twenty-four statues of the most distinguished Italians. On the right hand side of the gallery of exit, there is a statue of Columbus which as a work of art is excellent, but as to resemblance is absolutely worthless, and from descriptions I have read of it and information imparted to me by a most competent person, it is purely imaginary.

PAVIA BUST.—There is also in the University of Pavia, which it is pretended was the *Alma Mater* of Columbus, a beautiful colossal marble bust of the Discoverer. The hair is arranged in a fashion that did not prevail at the time of Columbus ; the lineaments of the face are, however, in accordance with the Capriolo and Cancellieri engravings. It is truly admirable as a work of art. (Cut No. 51.)

CAPITOLINE MUSEUM.—In the Capitoline Museum at Rome, there is a bust of Columbus of great artistic merit but of no historical value, as it is entirely imaginary. There is a reproduction of this bust in the Hall of the Historical Society of New York.

STATUE BY VINCENZO VELA. COLUMBUS IN AMERICA.—This colossal marble group was exhibited at the Paris Exposition in 1867. It represents the Admiral attired in a somewhat quaint and cumbersome dress, in the act of extending his hand over a young Indian maiden typifying America. I have read that it is a beautiful work of art, but historically worthless.

REVELLI STATUE.—This group is nothing more than a duplicate of that exhibited at the Paris Exposition of 1857, and which is elsewhere described as having been erected at Lima ; it is very well known, as there is a beautiful engraving of it by Desmaison, which has had a wide circulation. I do not know the present site of the statue, but it was sold at a high price.

FRANCE.

THE PARIS STATUE —There is in the Champs Élysées, at Paris, a statue by Cordier, which is much admired for its artistic merit. I will not describe it because it is a duplicate of the statue, by the same artist, surmounting the monument in the capital of the Republic of Mexico.

SPAIN.

SEVILLE.—In the court-yard of the old Exchange or Casa de Contratacion de las Indias, at Seville, where the Archives of the Indies are deposited, a small marble statue of Columbus has been erected. Its artistic merit is not great, and its value as a portrait even less.

CARTUJA OF SEVILLE.—The Dowager Marchioness of Pickman, has erected in the old building of the Cartuja, which is at present the most celebrated manufactory of ceramics in Spain, a monument in memory of Columbus, over the spot where his remains were once interred. The base of this monument is of encaustic tiles manufactured on the spot. From it rises a pedestal of Carrara marble surmounted by a colossal statue of the Admiral. He is represented with his right hand resting on a globe, placed on a column, and holding a scroll of parchment in his left hand. On the front of the monument is a memorial slab with the following inscription :

A – CRISTÓBAL COLÓN – EN MEMORIA DE – HABER ESTADO DEPOSITADAS-SUS CENIZAS DESDE EL AÑO MDXIII A MDXXXVI EN LA IGLESIA DE ESTA -CARTUJA- DE SANTA MARIA-DE LAS CUEVAS LA MARQUESA VIUDA DE PICKMAN – ERIGIO ESTE MONUMENTO-EN MDCCCLXXXVII. The interpretation of which is :

To CHRISTOPHER COLUMBUS, IN MEMORY OF HIS REMAINS HAVING BEEN DEPOSITED HERE FROM THE YEAR MDXIII TO MDXXXVI IN THE CHURCH OF THIS CARTUJA OF SANTA MARIA, THIS MONUMENT HAS BEEN ERECTED BY THE DOWAGER MARCHIONESS OF PICKMAN IN MDCCCLXXXVII.

MONUMENT AT SALAMANCA.—At Valcuerbo, near Salamanca, Columbus was entertained by Diego de Deza, prior of the great Dominican convent of San Esteban, while the Junta of Spanish ecclesiastics considered his projects. The

small farm-house still stands at a distance of about three miles west of Sala
manca, and there is a tradition among the peasants that on the crest of a small
hill in the vicinity of the house, now called, " *Teso de Colon*," (Columbus'
Peak), Columbus used to confer with his advisers or pass the time in solitary
meditation.   A monument has been erected by the present owner, Don Martin
de Solis.   It consists of a stone pyramid surmounted by a globe.

MONUMENT AT GRANADA.—The Spanish government, with the view of
commemorating the celebration of the Columbus Centennial, ordered the
erection of a monument at Granada, in honor of Isabella and Columbus, thus
uniting two of the most important events in the history of Spain: the conquest of
Granada which ended the rule of the Moors in the Peninsula, and the discovery
of America.   The artist selected to design and erect this splendid monument
was the young but famous sculptor, Mariano Benlliure, a native of Valencia,
and whose works have gained for him a great reputation in the art world.

The monument consists of three parts: the base, the pedestal, and the
group which crowns it.   The base is of marble from the quarries of Sierra
Elvira, near Granada, and consists of five wide low steps.   On the center of this
base stands the pedestal, which is a massive, rectangular structure, rich and
severe in character, and truly monumental.   Its corners are formed by four
plain pilasters, with a capital in the style of the Renaissance.   On the sides of
the pedestal are two large bass-reliefs, one of which represents a battle at Velez
Malaga, and the other the signing of the agreement between Columbus and the
Catholic Kings.   The names of prominent persons celebrated in Arms, Literature or the Church, attached to the court of the Catholic Kings, are inscribed
all over the pedestal.   In the front face are two allegorical figures representing
Granada and America, in the act of raising a tapestry covering the plinth, on
which are inscribed January 2, 1492, the date of the surrender of Granada,
and October 12, 1492, the date of the discovery of America, and beneath this
are the names of the principal supporters of Columbus, Fray Juan Pérez,
Cardinal Mendoza, Alonso de Quintanilla, Fray Hernando de Talavera, the
Marchioness of Moya and Luis de Santángel.

The tapestry which falls over the plinth, reaches to the top of the pedestal,
on which is the Queen seated on a magnificent Gothic chair, listening to the
plans of Columbus who is standing in front of her.   The ornamentation of the
sculptures on the plinth and the upper part of the monument give it a beautiful appearance and the figures in the bass-reliefs are magnificently executed.
The attire of the figures of Columbus and Isabella are faithfully copied from
monuments and descriptions.   According to native critics, the whole work is
an honor to modern Spanish art.

MONUMENT AT HUELVA.—From *The Centenario*, an illustrated review published in Madrid, I take the following details regarding the monument recently erected at Huelva. It consists of three parts: a base, nineteen feet in height, terminating in a spacious platform, to which access is obtained by three well-proportioned perrons, and from which a magnificent view is had of the Bar of Saltes, Huelva, Palos, Moguer and the sea. On this platform is erected a hexagonal pedestal seventy-three feet in height, ornamented by the prows of the three caravels; on this pedestal again stands a column, eighty-two feet in height, in the interior of which there is a winding staircase by means of which visitors can ascend to a gallery on a level with the vessels' prows, and have a splendid view of the surrounding country. The capital of the column is a group of savages which upholds it. The cornice is a representation of the diadem of the Catholic Kings, above which is a globe fifty feet in diameter, with a large cross as a finial. On the equator of this globe are inscribed the names of Columbus and Isabella, and on the lower part of the column are the names of all the persons who cooperated in the accomplishment of the undertaking either by their personal help or influence. Among them will be the names of all the members of the crews of the three caravels which have been handed down to posterity.

The monument is of white marble two hundred and five feet in height, and was designed by Ricardo Velasquez; the construction has been carried on under his supervision by the able architect, Hernandez Rubio. It stands in the center of a circular plaza, four hundred and eighty-five feet in diameter and two hundred and seven feet above the level of the sea, profusely ornamented with American plants. It was dedicated on August 3rd, 1892. (Cut No. 52.)

MONUMENT AT BARCELONA.—This is the noblest monument yet erected to the memory of Columbus, and just as that at Genoa, is really deserving of something more than a passing notice.

Barcelona is the place where the Catholic Kings received Columbus on his return from his first voyage, but nobody had ever thought of erecting a memorial to him there, until 1856, when a public-spirited Catalonian, Antonio Fajas, proposed to organize a general subscription for raising the funds required to defray the cost of the monument.

The projector was neither an artist nor even an educated man; he was simply a shoemaker, who having found that his trade was not lucrative enough for his ambition, enlisted in the army, and was sent to Cuba; after having obtained his discharge, he embarked in business and made a great fortune, which soon after his return to Barcelona, he lost in a banking venture; he

52—MONUMENT AT HUELVA.

left his country once more and commenced to work anew. He made another fortune and then returned to Barcelona, where he settled for good, always taking a lively interest in any scheme which he considered likely to further the glory and beauty of his native city.

He had always been an enthusiastic admirer of Columbus and in 1856, he proposed to the Municipal Council of his city, the erection of a great memorial to the Discoverer, to be entirely the work of Catalonian artists; but in consequence of political troubles very little attention was paid to his project. At last, in 1872, he found an enthusiastic supporter in the Mayor of the city, Rius y Taulet. Unforeseen obstacles prevented the carrying out of the work, notwithstanding a competition had been opened and proposals submitted. In 1881, Mr. Rius y Taulet was again elected Mayor of Barcelona, and urged by Fajas, he took the project in hand and opened a public subscription to defray the expenses. The sum of $200,000 was required and the greater part of it was raised in four years; the deficit, $24,000, was covered by the Provincial Deputation of Barcelona, which contributed $14,000, and by the Municipality of the same city, which donated $10,000.

Spanish artists exclusively, were invited to compete. Twenty-eight artists presented their designs and reports and the first prize was awarded to Mr. Cayetano Buigas Monraba, a distinguished Catalonian architect, who was charged with the direction of the work. The corner-stone was laid on Sept. 28th, 1882. Six years were required for the completion of the work, which was dedicated with great solemnity and in the presence of an immense concourse of people on the first day of June, 1888. (Cut No. 53.)

Seven Spanish and forty-nine foreign men-of-war, belonging to the American, Austrian, British, Dutch, French, German, Italian, Portuguese and Russian Navies participated in the dedication of this monument. The Queen-Regent of Spain with the royal family and a large number of prominent citizens assisted at the ceremonies.

Buigas called to his aid a galaxy of distinguished Catalonian artists, and apportioned the different parts of the work among them, using the greatest discretion in the selection of the men who were to realize his conceptions.

In giving a description of this truly majestic monument, I will divide it into five parts:

1. The Substructure or Stylobate; 2. The Base; 3. The Pedestal; 4. The Column; 5. The Statue.

The stylobate is in the form of a circle sixty-six feet in diameter, and is built of freestone; it is about four feet above the level of the Square; it is broken by four staircases twenty feet wide, each flanked by two lions, one

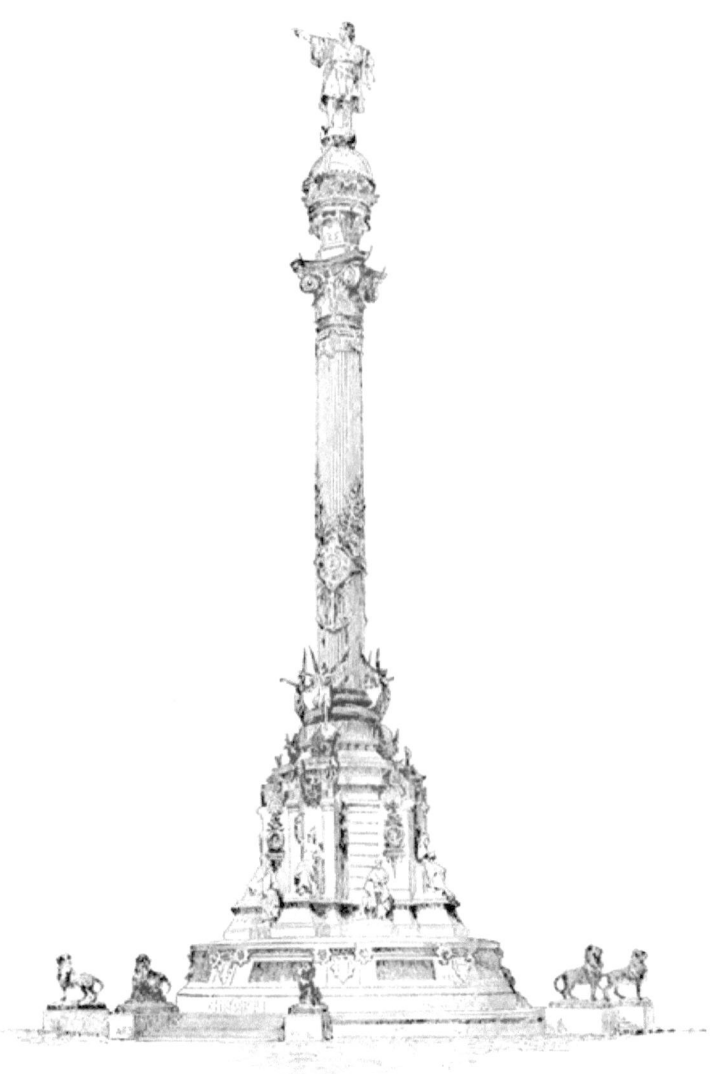

53—MONUMENT AT BARCELONA.

standing and one couchant. These eight magnificent and gigantic lions are
cast in bronze by the eminent master Vallmitjana, a son and able disciple
of Venancio Vallmitjana, the sculptor of the beautiful statue of "Columbus
in Chains."

2. The Base.—On this stylobate rises the base in the form of a truncated
cone. It is about thirteen feet high by fifty-nine feet in diameter at the foot.
It is built of enormous ashlers from the quarries of Monjuich. Embedded in
its sides there are eight bronze high reliefs representing the most important
incidents in the career of the Admiral :

1. Arrival of Columbus at the Convent of La Rábida ;
2. Conference at Salamanca :
3. Presentation of Columbus to the Catholic Kings at Cordova ;
4. Conference of Columbus and the Catholic Kings at Santa Fé :
5. Embarkation at Palos ;
6. Landing at Guanahani ;
7. Columbus taking possession of the New World in the name of the
Catholic Kings ;
8. Reception of Columbus at Barcelona by the Catholic Kings.

These high-reliefs are the work of the renowned artists, Llimosa and Pastor.

Alternating with the high-reliefs are the bronze coats of arms of the different
nations, which by their union constituted the Spanish Kingdom.

3. The Pedestal.—The beautiful pedestal is entirely allegorical of the
persons who helped Columbus in his enterprise. It is in the form of a cross
inserted in a polygon of eight sides, of which four are projecting. In the faces
there are eight large bronze medallions representing the following persons :
Ferdinand, Isabella, Fray Juan Perez, Fr. Antonio de Marchena, Vicente
Pinzon, Martin Alonso Pinzon, the Marquise de Moya, and Andres Cabrera.
In front of the receding sides stand four colossal groups in bronze : 1. The
Treasurer, Santángel, accompanied by a page to whom he hands a casket, (by
Ganot). 2. The cosmographer, Jaime de Blanes, with a page supporting a
globe, (by Pagés). 3. Captain Pedro Margarit triumphing over an Indian, (by
Alentorn). 4. Father Boyl preaching to an Indian kneeling before him, (by
Fuxá. It is a very curious fact that among the four persons honored in
these groups are two of the most inveterate enemies of Columbus, Captain
Margarit and Father Boyl. A little higher up, alternating with these groups
and in the abutting sides of the cross, are four splendid, colossal, seated
bronze statues, representing Catalonia by Carbonell, Aragon by Ganot, Castille
by Carcassó, and Leon by Atché.

4. The Column, which is a beautiful and original conception, stands on

54—STATUE ON THE BARCELONA MONUMENT.

this pedestal. It is a magnificent shaft of cast iron which at a distance seems to belong to the Corinthian order, but the capital is something completely different, as will be seen hereinafter. The shaft weighs thirty-two tons without the capital and was cast by Wohlgemuth. At the foot of the column are four beautiful winged figures of Fame holding a wreath of laurel in each hand and proclaiming the glory of Columbus. They are the work of the distinguished sculptor, Rosendo Nobas. At about one-third of the height of the column is a large medallion with the words, " BARCELONA A COLON." The capital is a magnificent piece of work. Europe, Asia, Africa, and America are represented allegorically as doing homage to Columbus, and by their side is the coat of arms granted to the Admiral by the Catholic Kings.

The capital is surmounted by the princely crown of Catalonia, and the crest of the crown is formed by a hemisphere allegorical of the Discovery. Around the crown there is a balcony to which visitors are carried by an elevator which runs in the column. The capital is all of bronze, and a part of it is cast from the thirty tons of old bronze presented for this purpose by the Spanish government to the City of Barcelona. The capital as well as the crown and hemisphere are the work of the eminent artist, Pastor.

On this capital, rises the magnificent statue of the Admiral, the work of the illustrious sculptor, Atché, to whom it was awarded in a competition with the no less illustrious Vallmitjana. It stands on a round socle, on which is inscribed the word, " TIERRA," (" LAND,") and represents the Admiral at the moment of descrying land in the far distance, pointing to it with the right hand and holding in the left a chart or parchment. The position is strikingly majestic with the right foot advanced and resting on the left. He is represented as simply but richly attired as Admiral of the Indies in court dress, and exactly in accordance with the fashion of his times. His uncovered head is of the Jovian type, softened, with long hair flowing over the shoulders. The engraving of the monument is copied from a beautiful photograph which I owe to the kindness of my friend, the distinguished writer, Mr. Arturo Cuyás, and the engraving representing the statue as also the full history and description and many illustrations of the monument are found in the *Ilustracion* of Barcelona, (Sept. 23rd, 1888), and the *Ilustracion* of Madrid, (Sept. 22nd, 1888), which have been kindly placed at my disposal by the able artist, Mr. Juan Romeu y Solá ; both are Catalonians, and highly esteemed residents of this city.

The statue is also of bronze and measures eight mètres (26" 3' English measurement). It was cast in two halves by Vidal at a very large cost, and after five months of constant toil, but with the most complete success.

The height of the whole monument from the level of the famous Rambla,

55—STATUE BY SAN MARTIN AT MADRID.

of Barcelona, where it stands to the top of the statue, is 57, 20 mètres, equivalent to about 187½ English feet.

The monument is entirely Spanish : it was raised with Spanish money exclusively, to such a degree, that the President of the United States and the King of Italy, having expressed a desire to take part in the subscription, their offers were politely declined. The iron, steel, bronze, stone and lime employed in its construction are all Spanish, and the conception, direction and handiwork of every one of its parts is not only all Spanish, but exclusively Catalonian. Undoubtedly, Barcelona has a right to boast of having erected in honor of the great Admiral, the most beautiful, noble, rich and artistic of all the memorials yet raised by human hands in memory of Columbus, as those of Genoa, Madrid, Mexico and New York, cannot for a moment bear comparison with that of the capital of the Principality of Catalonia.

MADRID. STATUE BY SAN MARTIN.—In the Court of the Colonial Office (Ministerio de Ultramar), at Madrid, a colossal statue of Columbus has been erected. It is the work of the famous Spanish sculptor José San Martin, a disciple of Ponciano Ponzano, and is one of the most beautiful statues of Columbus. Added to its great artistic merit is the closeness with which the descriptions of Columbus have been followed, and the accuracy of the details of the dress. Columbus is represented in the costume of Admiral of the Indies, carrying the standard of Castile ; behind him is a globe. The features of the statue are very much like the portrait at the Naval Museum, and reproductions have frequently been made in reduced size for different localities in Spain and Spanish America. (See cut No. 55.)

NAVAL MUSEUM. MADRID.—The second saloon of the Naval Museum at Madrid bears the name of Sala de Colon (Columbus Hall), a large bust of the Admiral is its principal ornament, but according to what I have been told, it is a work of very indifferent merit, from a historical point of view, as it is entirely imaginary, though as a work of art it is very effective.

THE MONUMENT IN MADRID.—I translate from *The Centenario* of Madrid, the following description of the monument to the Discoverer, erected there :

" In commemoration of so conspicuous an event as the marriage of the never-to-be-forgotten King Alphonso XII., to Maria Christina, the present Queen-Regent of Spain, the Spanish nobility determined to start a subscription for the purpose of erecting a monument at this Court, to the glorious discoverer of the New World. In the competition opened for the purpose of carrying out this project, the famous artist Arturo Mélida, submitted a design which strongly attracted public attention, on account of the originality of the conception, as he proposed that the memorial should assume the form of a vessel.

MADRID. 2600 — Monumento de Colón en Recoletos.

56—MONUMENT AT MADRID.

No award having been made in the first competition, a second was opened in which the conditions of the work were set forth very explicitly, and the specifications under which the monument should be constructed, and exacting among some others as an essential one, that it should consist of a pillar with a base. In this second competition, Mr. Mélida again took part, and to him was awarded the prize, namely : the execution of the work.

" The material of the monument is Novelda stone, and it stands in the center of a square named after the immortal Genoese. It is composed of two parts: a square base with an octagonal pillar, which is surmounted by a statue of Italian marble, one of the masterpieces of the famous sculptor, Jeronimo Suñol. The base is enriched with allegories, detached statues and other details, which are in the best artistic taste.

" The high-reliefs which adorn the four faces are of excellent design, and of exquisite workmanship. The one in the front represents the famous vessel, the Santa Maria ; on the deck of the historical ship is seen a hemisphere with the new continent, and a band on which is inscribed in monachal characters, the motto: 'POR CASTILLA, Y POR LEON, NUEVO MUNDO HALLO COLON.' The high-relief on the north side shows the image of Our Lady of the Pillar, with the ever memorable date of the discovery of America, *12 de Octubre de 1492*, at her feet, and the names of the intrepid Spaniards who followed Columbus in his marvellous enterprise. On the eastern face is depicted the touching scene of the offer of her jewels made by Isabella I., for the purpose of raising funds for the forsaken and daring navigator ; while on the western one is a representation of the conference at which Columbus revealed his adventurous plans to Father Deza.

" Four heralds or kings-at-arms, of life size, and wearing emblazoned dalmatics, stand at the angles of the base, on addorsed pillars, under elegant canopies consisting of small groined vaults, carved in the form of polygonal capitals, surrounded by festooned, pendant arches, and crowned by pinnacles. Above this, is a circular arcade, between the columns of which are seen four coats of arms of Spain, supported by the eagle of St. John the Evangelist ; above this part, rises a pillar ornamented by beautiful mouldings on which is the figure of Columbus, standing in a stately attitude, holding the standard of Castile in his right hand. The monument is surrounded by an iron railing and stands in the center of a garden.

"The style of this remarkable work is Gothic of the third period, better known as the *florid* or *flamboyant*. This name originated from the filling of the open spaces with fanciful traceries, imitating the fibres of leaves with small interlaced columns and arches forming undulations. The style cannot be more characteristic, or recall to us more perfectly, the taste which prevailed at the time of the Catholic Kings.

"The entire monument, with the exception of the statue, which is the work of Mr. Suñol, is the original design of Mr. Mélida, which in this case as on every former occasion, when his artistic talent has been put to the test, has added a fresh leaf to his glorious crown, especially showing his profound knowledge, and endorsing the good judgment of those who entrusted him with the direction of the work of restoration in San Juan de los Reyes."

I will further add that the statue is worthy of more than such a passing notice. It represents the Admiral—as has already been stated—standing beside a capstan on which there is a globe, and holding the standard of Castile in his right hand, while he extends the left, and raises his head as if in the act of thanking Heaven for his glorious victory.

The details of the statue are excellent ; the features being in exact accordance with the historical descriptions, and appear to have been taken from the picture in the Naval Museum at Madrid. The material of the statue is white Carrara marble, and it is 14 feet in height. I will state in conclusion that according to the photograph by Laurent, in my possession, the coat of arms of Columbus is beneath the globe, and the inscription reads: " A CASTILLA Y A LEÓN, NUEVO MUNDO DIÓ COLON," instead of " POR CASTILLA Y POR LEÓN, NUEVO MUNDO HALLÓ COLON," as is stated in the article I have translated.

WATLING'S ISLAND.

In 1891, an expedition was sent out by the *Chicago Herald* to find the landing-place of Columbus. After very careful investigation and inquiry, the party erected a monument fifteen feet high on Watling's Island, which bears the following inscription :

ON THIS SPOT CHRISTOPHER COLUMBUS FIRST SET FOOT ON
THE SOIL OF THE NEW WORLD.
ERECTED BY THE CHICAGO HERALD
JUNE 15, 1891.

NASSAU.

STATUE AT NASSAU.—In front of the Government House at Nassau, Bahama Islands, is a statue of Christopher Columbus. It is nine feet high and stands on a six foot pedestal, on the north face of which is inscribed :

COLUMBUS. 1492.

It was a gift to the colony, by Sir James Carmichael Smyth, Governor of the Bahamas from 1829-1833, was modeled in London in 1831, is of metal painted white, and was erected in May, 1832. According to the opinion of some friends who have seen it, it has neither artistic nor historic value.

CUBA.

STATUE IN THE COURT-YARD OF THE CAPTAIN-GENERAL'S PALACE AT HAVANA.—There is in the court yard of the Captain-General's Palace at Havana, a large marble statue of Columbus (cut No. 57), which is the work of the well-known sculptor, Garbeille. He has taken as his model, the picture in the Naval Museum at Madrid. The statue, which is not lacking in artistic merit, formerly stood in the center of the Park at Havana. It occupied the site of the statue of Isabella II., which was removed after the revolution of September, 1868. On the return of the Bourbons to Spain, this statue, which is the work of the same artist, was restored to its former place in the Park, and that of Columbus was relegated to the court-yard of the Captain-General's Palace, which is the worst position, from an artistic point of view, which could have been chosen, as it is surrounded by walls and trees and is almost in front of the stables.

STATUE IN THE TEMPLETE.—In the city of Havana, there is a small, tasteful building erected in commemoration of the first mass said in Havana, in 1517: this building is known as the Templete. There is in it a marble bust of the Admiral, which occupies a small niche. It is the gift of the famous and venerated Bishop, José Diaz Espada y Landa. The bust was placed there in 1828, but I have not been able to learn the name of the artist, and I have not

57—STATUE AT HAVANA.

taken great interest in it. It has absolutely no merit either artistic or historic. It is surrounded by an iron railing and looks as is generally remarked in Havana, as if the Admiral were there in prison.

VALLMITJANA. STATUE OF COLUMBUS IN CHAINS. HAVANA, SOCIEDAD ECONOMICA.—This beautiful work, by the most distinguished of modern Spanish sculptors, is only a model in clay. It was bought by the patriotic Cuban Deputy, Gabriel Millet, and presented by him to the Sociedad Economica of Havana, a Society which has always been foremost in all matters tending to promote the welfare and progress of the Island of Cuba. (Cut 58.)

It represents Columbus as a man of sixty years of age; the head is superb in sentiment and expression. He is seated on a coil of rope on the deck of the ship, which is carrying him to Spain in chains. over that same Sea of Darkness, which he had unveiled. He reclines against a capstan, in an attitude which shows his fetters. Notwithstanding the fact that capstans of that form were not known at the time, the slight anachronism only adds to the general beautiful effect of the work. His features agree with the description left by his contemporaries. The expression of the face is a sublime combination of suffering, melancholy and resignation. A profound knowledge of anatomy is shown in the details of the emaciated face and hands. The inscription on the base is as follows:

CRISTOBAL COLON,

POR EL ESCULTOR ESPAÑOL, D. V. VALLMITJANA,

DONADO A LA REAL SOCIEDAD ECONÓMICA DE LA HABANA,

POR DON GABRIEL MILLET,

1881.

HAVANA MONUMENT.—A monument in the memory of Columbus is being erected at Havana, Cuba. The most striking feature of which is a terrestrial globe encircled by a band, on which are the words, " Non plus ultra," which, as is well known, was the motto of Spain at the time of the discovery. Beneath this globe is a lion tearing off the three first letters with a blow of his paw, representing the negative idea, showing by this allegory that there is a " Plus ultra," as evidenced by the discovery of a New World. (Cut No. 59.)

The globe stands on a truncated pyramid, resting on a quadrangular base, flanked by four statues standing at the four salient sides. These statues represent Courage, Study, History and Navigation. To this last figure, a child is presenting a compass. On each of the panels is a bass-relief representing a notable event in the history of the discovery.

The first of these bass-reliefs shows the cell of Father Juan Perez in the Convent of the Rábida, in which Columbus is depicted as explaining his plans

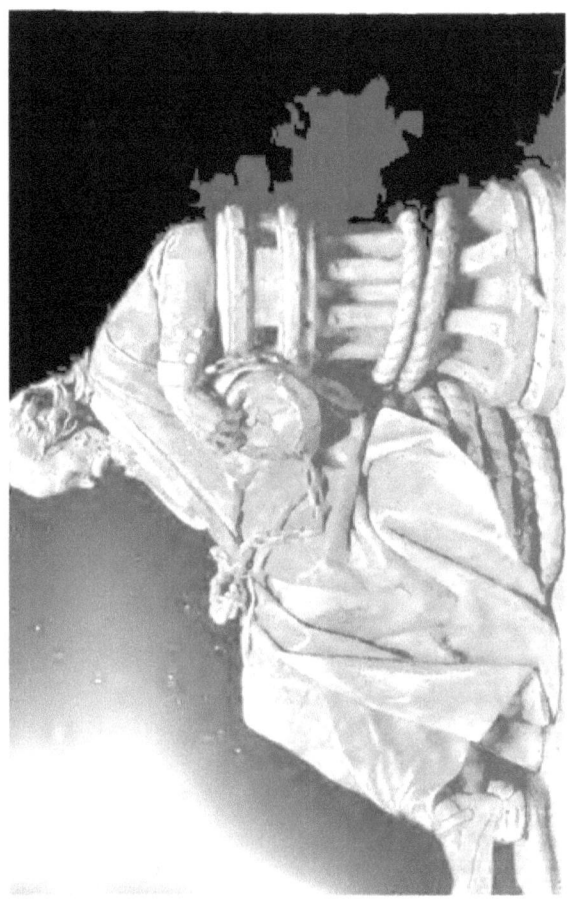

to the Franciscan Prior, to Garci Fernandez and to other monks of the Convent.
The second represents the departure of Columbus; he stands in the center,
receiving the benediction of the friendly Prior. The third is a graphic picture
of the landing at San Salvador, the Admiral standing in the center, his

59—MONUMENT AT HAVANA.

followers kneeling at his feet, kissing his hands and the hem of his robe, and
asking his pardon; the fourth is the reception of Columbus at Barcelona by
the Catholic Kings, in which Ferdinand is rising to receive the Admiral and
his suite, two members of which are Indians, male and female. The four bass-

reliefs are of beautiful design. On the side opposite to that on which the lion is shown tearing off the word "*non*," an eagle with open wings displays the escutcheon of the Spanish nation, then in use.

On another of the sides of the pyramid, is an artistic medallion with the busts of the Catholic Kings resting on one of the wings of the eagle, and on

60- TOMB IN THE CATHEDRAL AT HAVANA.

the opposite side is a medallion representing the sail of a ship, with the standard of the Holy Virgin and Child.

Another nautical design is on the top of the monument showing a barge battered by the winds and waves, surmounting the globe. On this barge stands Faith, guiding Christopher Columbus, as a symbol that the New World has been discovered under the *ægis* of the Cross.

The sculptor, Antonio Susillo, though still a young man, is one of the most famous Spanish artists. His model obtained the first prize in the competition for the design for this monument, and he will receive $100,000 for building it in accordance with his plans. It is 60 feet high and is now in course of construction. It will be erected on a most beautiful site in the Capital of Cuba, in the Park opposite the Tacon Theatre.

All these statues and bass-reliefs will be of bronze ; the monument will be fifty-two and a half feet in height ; the group on the top will be twenty-three feet : the lion twelve feet, the eagle twelve feet ; the four bass-reliefs ten feet in length, and the four statues which are all seated, will be ten feet each in height.

THE NEW SEPULCHRE OF COLUMBUS IN THE CATHEDRAL OF HAVANA.— This is in actual course of construction in Spain. The originator of the project and director of the work is Mr. Arthur Mélida, a very celebrated Spanish sculptor. (Cut No. 60.)

The monument will be of bronze and marble ; the base is composed of enormous ashlers of gray marble from the quarries of Alconera, on which will be a plinth of black Belgian marble, consisting of five pieces.

Four heralds dressed in full court mourning upbear the sarcophagus ; they bear respectively the arms of Castile, Léon, Aragon, and Navarre, the four nations which united under the rule of Ferdinand and Isabella, constituted the kingdom of Spain.

The sarcophagus is of bronze, ornamented with enamelled metallic plates, and in it will be placed the pretended remains of Columbus now at Havana.

THE HAVANA HIGH-RELIEF.—A large marble slab on the right hand side of the Presbytery in the Cathedral at Havana, marks the resting place of the supposed remains of Columbus, brought there on board of the ship of the line, the "San Lorenzo," on the 15th of February, 1796, by Gen. Aristizaval.

It represents Columbus in armor with a ruff and holding a globe. It strongly resembles the Cladera and Muñoz pictures, and as stated elsewhere in this work is almost an exact copy of the Vasquez engraving (*q. v.*) (Cut No. 61.)

The execution of the high-relief is beautiful. It is a half-length in an oval frame ; on the upper part is a garland of laurel and oak leaves. In a square beneath the medallion are carved a number of nautical emblems, and above this on a smaller slab is the following inscription : O! RESTOS E IMAGEN DEL GRANDE COLON – MIL SIGLOS DURAD GUARDADAS EN LA URNA – Y EN LA REMEMBRANZA DE NUESTRA NACION !– the translation of which is :– Oh ! Remains and Image of Great Columbus, Rest in

Peace for a Thousand Centuries in this Urn and in the Remembrance of our Nation!

The supposed remains are in a niche behind the slab, and on the metallic receptacle enclosing them is the following Latin epitaph composed by Bishop

61—HIGH RELIEF — CATHEDRAL, HAVANA.

Tres Palacios :-D. O. M.-CLARIS. HEROS LIGUSTIN.-CHRISTOPHORUS COLUMBUS- A SE, REI NAUTIC. SCIENT. INSIGN. - NOV. ORB. DE-TECT.- ATQUE CASTELL. ET LEGION. REGIB. SUBJECT.- VALLISOL. OCCUB.- XIII KAL. JUN. A. MDVI-CARTUSIANOR. HISPAL.-CADAV.

CUSTOD. TRADIT.–TRANSFER. NAM IPSE PRESCRIPS.– IN HISPA-
NIOLÆ METROP. ECC. HINC PACE SANCIT, GALLIÆ REIPUBLCÆ
SESS.–IN HANC V.MAR. CONCEPT. IMM. CATH. OSSA TRANS.–MAXIM.
OM. ORD. FREQUENT. SEPULT. MAND – XV KAL. FEB. A. MDCCXCVI.
–HAVAN. CIVIT.–TANT. VIR. MERITOR. IN SE NON. IMMEM. EXUV.
IN OPTAT. DIEM TUITUR– HOCCE MONUM. EREX.– PRESUL. ILL. D.
D. PHILIPPO JPH. TRES PALACIOS– CIVIC. AC MILITAR. REI. GEN.
PR.EF. EXMO.– D. D. LUDOVICO DE LAS CASAS.– The translation of
this is :– "D. O. M. The Illustrious Genoese Hero Christopher Columbus,
Renowned For His Nautical Knowledge, By Himself Discovered a New World
And Gave It To The Kings Of Castille And Leon– Died at Valladolid In The
Year MDVI, The Body Being Entrusted To The Care Of the Carthusians Of
Seville, Was Transferred As He Himself Prescribed, To The Metropolitan
Church Of Hispaniola– Hence Peace Being Concluded And The Island Ceded
To France. The Frequently Buried Remains Were Given Burial In The Pres-
ence Of An Immense Concourse Of All Classes, On The Kalends Of The XVth
Of February In The Year MDCCXCVI.– The City Of Havana Unwilling That
So Great And Meritorious a Man Should Be Forgotten And To Guard His
Precious Remains On This Auspicious Day Erects This Monument."

The Most Illustrious D. D. Philip Jph. Tres Palacios, Bishop– And The
Most Excellent D. D. Ludovico De Las Casas Captain-General Of The Civil
And Military Government."

The remains will be transferred to the new monument for the Cathedral,
which has been described in its proper place.

MELERO: STATUE OF COLUMBUS FOR THE TOWN OF COLON, CUBA.—This
beautiful statue to be erected in the centre of the Park of Isabella the Catholic,
at Colon, in the Island of Cuba, is the work of a talented Cuban painter,
Miguel Melero, Director of the Academy of Painting and Sculpture, at Havana.

The whole monument will be 28 feet in height. The pedestal rises on a
wide flight of steps, forming an octagonal prism, with a plain capital on which
stands the statue. (Cut No. 62.)

From the projecting faces are four detached pillars, and four bronze lions
modelled by the same artist. The front face will bear a commemorative inscription on a bronze slab.

The statue is of bronze, about eight feet in height and represents Columbus
leaning on an anchor and a capstan, pointing to the newly discovered land :
the model in clay, has been exhibited, and has met with universal approval.
The artist has faithfully followed the descriptions of Columbus, and the dress,
anchor and capstan are historically correct.

63.—STATUE AT COLON, CUBA.   115

The bronze for the statue has been donated by the planters of the District of Colon, and the statue has just been successfully cast in the foundry of the town of Colon, by Messrs. Armstrong & Estapé.

The monument will be enclosed by a bronze chain depending from eight pillars of artistic design.

63— STATUE AT CARDENAS

THE CARDENAS STATUE.—In the Plaza de Recreo in the city of Cárdenas, there is a bronze statue of Columbus which was erected on the 25th of December, 1862. (Cut No. 63.) The model was made in Madrid by the eminent

Valencian sculptor, Francisco Piquer, following the conception of Mr. Caveda, of the Academy of History. It was cast in bronze at Marseilles by Morell. The hero is represented attired in a very modest garb, lifting the veil that covers a part of the globe with the left hand, and pointing with the right, to the regions discovered by him. In the front face of the pedestal, there is a very beautiful bass-relief representing the triumph of Faith and Hell vanquished by the victory that Columbus obtained by his discovery. On the back of the pedestal, there is an inscription which runs as follows:

OCCIDUARUM REGIONUM INVENTOR GENUÆ DECORI MAXIMO HISPANIARUM ORNAMENTO E CUNCTO FERE LATO PATET TER RARUM ORBE INSOLENS PROPTER FACTUM DERISUM OLIM NUNC OMNIUM PLAUSUS, SANCTA CUM ADMIRATIONE EXTORQUENTI CHRISTOPHORUS COLUMBUS HOCCINI PIETATIS ERGO ET GRATI ANIMI INSIGNE MONUMENTUM SECUNDA ELIZABETHO REGNANTE OPPIDUM CARDENAS POSUIT ANNO MDCCCLXII.

The distinguished sculptor, Mr. Fernando Miranda, then a disciple of Piquer and now residing at New York, greatly helped him in modelling this beautiful work.

The statue in Mexico and that by Cordier in Paris, are almost exact copies of that by Piquer, in the city of Cárdenas, Cuba: the attitude in each being exactly alike, with the exception of the right arm, which in that by Piquer points to the newly discovered land, while in that of Cordier, it is raised in a triumphant manner.

CIFUENTES, CUBA.—Miss Felipa G. Lázaro, a young lady artist born at Madrid, Spain, and at present residing in Havana, has modeled a handsome bust about three feet high which is to be erected on a pedestal in the town of Cifuentes, Cuba.

The features, as far as I can judge from the cuts I have seen, are taken from the portrait in the Naval Museum, at Madrid. On the lower part of the bust is the coat of arms conferred upon Columbus by the Catholic Kings. Miss Lázaro is not only a sculptress, but also a painter of repute. She studied under the able sculptor Molinelli, as well as under the eminent Spanish water color painter, Lozana.

STATUE AT BAYAMO.—In the Plaza del Cristo, at Bayamo, Cuba, a small statue was erected on October 1892. From descriptions I have read, it is the work of the Messrs. Castells, and is a very beautiful piece of workmanship. A correspondent of the journal *La Union*, published at Manzanillo, says that it is unique in its class, as the material consists of the first earth trodden by Columbus in Cuba, and being painted white resembles Carrara marble. It appears therefore, that the statue is of clay, but as the question as to the first earth trodden by Columbus in Cuba has yet to be decided, I cannot say from whence the clay for the statue came.

For the greater part of the descriptions and pictures of the monuments in Cuba, I am indebted to the kindness of Mr. Carlos I. Párraga, a distinguished lawyer and resident of Havana.

SANTO DOMINGO

MONUMENT AT SANTO DOMINGO.—This statue was erected in 1886; its cost was defrayed by a public subscription instituted by the Municipal Council of the city of Santo Domingo. It stands in the centre of the principal square of the city, in the immediate vicinity of the Governor's palace. The pedestal is square, of pyramidal form, and the material is white marble. The statue is bronze, and of colossal size. The head of the Admiral as well as his attire in the garb of the navigators of his time are strictly historic. (Cut No. 64.)

On the pedestal of the statue and in the attitude of ascending to reach the Admiral, is an Indian female figure probably intended for Anacaona, the caciquess of Xaragua.

The inscription on the monument reads:

ILUSTRE Y ESCLARECIDO DON CRISTOVAL COLON.

The statue which was cast in France some years ago, stands in the centre of the Plaza facing the cathedral.

64—MONUMENT AT SANTO DOMINGO.

HONDURAS.

STATUE AT TRUJILLO.—The government of the Republic of Honduras has ordered the erection of a bronze statue of the Discoverer on a pedestal of granite, at the expense of the nation. Is was to be unveiled on the 12th of October 1892, and will stand in the centre of the Park of the city of Truxillo. On the front of the pedestal there is an inscription which reads as follows:— "La República de Honduras á Cristóbal Colón, 1492–1892," the translation of which is "The Republic of Honduras to Christopher Columbus."

COLOMBIA.

STATUE AT COLON. In 1866, Eugénie, Empress of the French, presented to Gen. Tomas Mosquera, ex-President of Colombia, and Minister at the French Court, this beautiful monument as a gift to the republic of which he was the representative. The present was formally accepted on the 29th day of June, of the same year, and was erected in 1870, in the city of Colon, in the new ward named Christopher Columbus, at the northern entrance to the Panama canal and where the buildings of the Company are situated. (Cut No. 65.)

This group was exhibited at the Paris Exposition of 1867 and was much admired. It is of bronze, of colossal size, and stands on a low square block of granite, which is entirely unpretentious, artistically. It represents Columbus in the uniform of an Admiral, wearing a rich mantle over his shoulders. The head is uncovered and he is raising an Indian girl who is half crouching before him. The head is superb and the artist has rigorously adhered to the descriptions we have of the Admiral.

On the face of the pedestal is the following incription :—

"CHRISTOPHORUS COLUMBUS EXTREMUM, INGENTEM, CÆCUM TRANS ÆQUORA MUNDUM, HESPERLE RATES DUXERAT: IPSE DEDIT. IV IDUS OCTOBRIS M.CCCCXCII."

On the back is another inscription reading :

"EL GRAN GENERAL TOMAS C. DE MOSQUERA PRESENTO AL CONGRESO DE LOS ESTADOS UNIDOS DE COLOMBIA ESTA ESTATUA, DON DE LA EMPARATRIZ DE LOS FRANCESES, EUGENIA."

65—STATUE AT COLON.

The statue was received at Panama, on May 1, 1870, but I have been unable to ascertain the date of its dedication.

MEXICO.

MONUMENT AT MEXICO. This monument is due entirely to the munificence of Mr. Antonio Escandon, a rich banker of Mexico. His nephew, Mr. Alejandro Arango y Escandon was entrusted by him with the selection of the artist and the persons to be represented in the monument.

Mr. Arango placed the work in the hands of Charles Cordier, the distinguished French sculptor, in 1873, and it was delivered to him at Vera Cruz, in 1875, but on account of some discussion about the selection of the site, it was not dedicated until August, 1877. It had been previously exhibited at the Palais de l'Industrie, Paris, and was much admired. The cost of the work was nearly $100,000. (Cut No. 66.)

The monument occupies a splendid site on the Calzada de la Reforma, which extends to Chapultepec. It is surrounded by a beautiful garden and is enclosed by posts and chains, so placed as to allow of a very close inspection of the monument and its details.

The form of the socle is octagonal, each side measuring about sixteen and one-half feet. At each of the angles, there is an ornamental bronze lamp post each of which has a cluster of five gas lights.

On the socle stands the base which is in the form of a square with truncated angles. The faces are adorned as follows:— on the east side are engraved the words, "A Cristobal Colon," and this inscription is bordered by four bronze bands set in the stone, surmounted by the coat of arms of Columbus and Castile, with a pomegranate beneath. There is a shorter inscription stating that the monument was dedicated in August, 1877. The west side is adorned with laurels and palms in bronze, and an ellipse containing a fragment of the letter of Columbus to Rafael Sanchez commencing, *"trigesima die . . . , ad cateras alias perrenimus."*

Under this ellipse is the dedication reading :—

"CHRISTOFORO COLUMBO, HOC ÆTERNÆ ADMIRATIONIS TESTIMONIUM EREGI URBIS MEXICANÆ OFFERERI VOLUIT. ANTONIUS ESCANDON. MDCCCLXXV."

On the south side there is a beautiful bass-relief in bronze, representing Columbus taking leave of Fray Juan Perez : in the background appear the Convent of La Rábida and the village of Palos.

On the north side is another bass-relief showing the Landing of Columbus Both possess great artistic merit and are about four and a half feet by about four feet two inches.

66—MONUMENT AT MEXICO.

At each of the truncated angles of this pedestal stands a bronze statue about seven feet two inches in height; they represent four monks, Fray Juan Perez, Las Casas, Deza and Gante. The first and the third named were personal friends of Columbus and warmly aided him in his enterprise. Las Casas is the well-known "Apostle of the Indians," and Gante was the founder of the first college in Mexico, in 1529. All are represented seated.

This pedestal is surmounted by one of similar design, and on it stands the colossal statue of Columbus in white marble; its height is twelve feet. He stands with his right hand extended towards heaven, as if giving thanks for his great discovery, while with his left hand he raises the veil which concealed the world he has just discovered.

The entire monument, which is forty-five feet high, is of Russian jasper and is a beautiful and noble structure; but the statue makes Columbus a young man and his features are not those so well-known from the description of his contemporaries.

For the data used in the foregoing description I am indebted to the kindness of Mrs. Helen S. Conant, a lady well-known in the literary world, and who has always taken a great interest in the history and literature of Spanish America.

PERU.

THE MONUMENT AT LIMA.—In the centre of the Plaza del Acho, in the Alameda del Acho in Lima, a splendid monument has been erected in memory of Columbus. On the beautiful pedestal which is surrounded by a railing of artistic design, and stands in a pretty garden, there is a colossal group in Italian marble, representing Columbus partially drawing aside his mantle with his right hand, and disclosing an Indian maiden typifying America, rising before him, while in his left hand, he holds a cross. Columbus is richly clad in the full dress of an Admiral, with an ample mantle and plumed cap. (Cut No. 67.)

The group, which is of great artistic merit, was exhibited at the Paris Exposition of 1867, where it obtained a prize, and is the work of the famous Italian sculptor, Salvatore Revelli. The four faces of the pedestal, which is of white marble, have beautiful bass-reliefs and inscriptions and are the work of the Italian artist, Giuseppe Palombini. At the four corners of the railings are

67—MONUMENT AT LIMA.

massive, square granite pillars, with bronze lion's heads on the sides, and dolphins and tridents in the same metal on the top of each.

This statue was erected in 1880. The features of the Admiral are in strict accordance with the descriptions we have of him, and his attire is that in vogue at the close of the XVIth century.

CHILI.

STATUE AT VALPARAISO.—A bronze statue standing on a marble pedestal has been erected at Valparaiso, Chili. The figure is of heroic size, and stands with the foot advanced, and a cross in the right hand.

BUST AT SANTIAGO.—At Santiago, Chili, is a marble bust of Columbus, following the De Bry type. The bust has a Dutch cap and garments.

UNITED STATES.

THE BOSTON STATUE.—One of the earliest statues erected to the memory of Columbus, in the United States, is that at Boston, presented to the city in 1849, by the resident Italian merchants; the chairman of the Presentation Committee being Mr. Iasigi. The site of the statue is on Louisburg Square; it is now in somewhat poor condition, and has no artistic merit.

BOSTON.—MONTEVERDE: THE INFANT COLUMBUS.—The illustrious Monteverde is the sculptor of this superb work, which represents Columbus as a charming child at play: he is sitting on a mooring-post upon a pier, against which the waves are breaking; he is in deep meditation and holds a book in his hand. I have in my possession only some cuts representing it from different points of view, and I have also seen a plaster cast of it. It is difficult to conceive a more graceful work, and although it has no historical value, its artistic merit has been a source of inspiration for many distinguished Italian poets. This statue first revealed to the world the genius of the artist and was the stepping stone to his brilliant career. It was made in Rome in 1871, and after winning a gold medal at an exhibition at Parma, Italy, was presented to the city of Boston by Mr. A. P. Chamberlain, of Concord, Mass.

THE NEW YORK MONUMENT.—The finest memorial of Columbus, in this
country, is the well-timed and graceful gift of the Italian residents of the

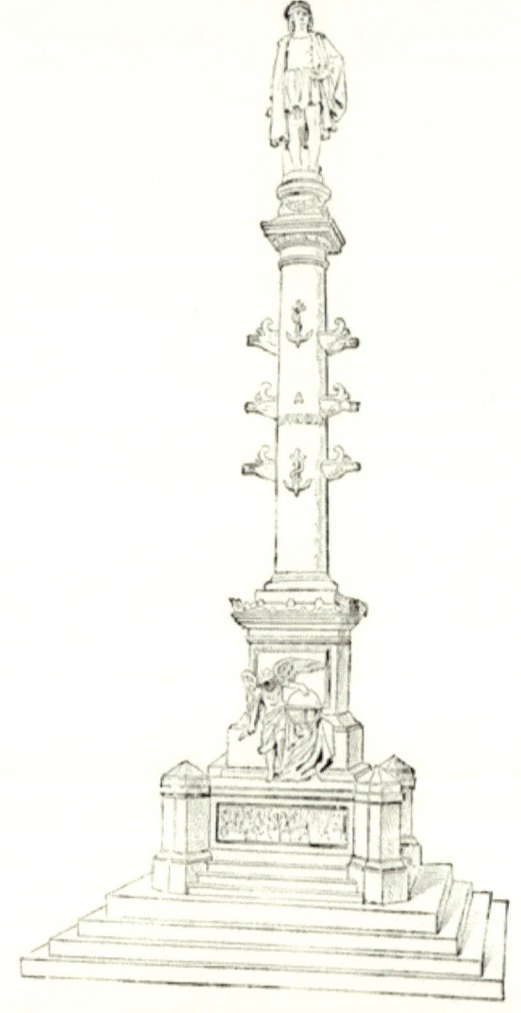

68—THE NEW YORK MONUMENT.

United States to the city of New York, which stands on the beautiful site
facing Central Park, at the corner of 59th Street and 8th Avenue. (Cut No. 68.)

This handsome monument to the immortal discoverer of America was formally dedicated with appropriate and imposing ceremonies, at which a vast crowd of the residents of New York and visitors from all parts of the United States assisted, on the 12th of October, 1892, the 400th anniversary of the discovery of this Continent.

It was in January, 1889, that the order for the designs was sent to the Minister of Public Instruction, Bosselli, through Signor Barsotti, editor and proprietor of *Il Progresso Italo-Americano*, by the Italian residents of New York. In accordance with the instructions, sculptors were invited to compete for the design of the monument, it being expressly stipulated that none but artists of Italian birth would be eligible. As the architecture as well as the design had to be passed upon, nine judges were appointed, three painters, three architects and three sculptors; the painters were Mascari, Prosperi and Marini; the architects were Calderini, who designed the new Palace of Justice at Rome, Sacconi and Basile: the sculptors were Monteverde, the artist who executed the Infant Columbus, Gallori and Ferrari. The award of the committee was given to the celebrated sculptor, Gaetano Russo, the designer of many works which are world-renowned. Russo was born at Messina, Sicily, but in 1848, when he was scarcely out of his teens, his enthusiastic love of art led him to Rome, where he was a pupil in the Academia dei Belle Arti, on leaving which institution, he became the pupil of Monteverde. He is in receipt of a handsome pension from Messina, his native city.

I will now give a description of the monument. It is seventy-seven feet high. The terraced pedestal and octagonal corner post are of red granite from Ravenna, against which the noble figure of Genius and the magnificent Alpine eagle, the strongest as well as the fiercest of all its family, on opposite sides of the second terrace of the pedestal are seen to the greatest advantage, both being of the purest marble from the celebrated quarries of Carrara. The ornamental capital of the column is also of marble, and the plain pedestal which is crowned with the marble statue of the great Admiral is of gray granite. The bass-reliefs below the Genius and at its sides are of bronze, as well as the six prows—three on each side of the column, and the anchors and central inscription —"A CRISTOFORO COLOMBO"—forming altogether a very beautiful combination of color and material. The size of the bass-reliefs is ten feet by two: the Genius is ten feet four inches in height. The figure of Columbus is twelve feet nine inches high. The Admiral is represented at the moment his vague ideas have assumed sure and definite shape. He stands proudly erect, his piercing gaze seeming even then to discern the marvelous discoveries that awaited him thousands of miles away. The ship's rudder grasped firmly in

his right hand, is emblematic of the solution of the great problem which he
has just conceived.   The anchors symbolize the merchant service, to which
his vessels, the Pinta, the Niña and the Santa Maria, belonged.   The Genius

69—BUST OF COLUMBUS, MIRANDA FOUNTAIN.

and the Eagle below the figure are magnificent in conception, design and
execution.

The bass-reliefs under the Genius and the Eagle, represent two supreme
moments in the life of the Admiral.   The ships, boats, banners and costumes
in both are fairly correct historically.   In the first of these bass-reliefs, Colum-

bus is depicted starting off in his boat, to step upon the newly discovered land, the sight of which has just gladdened the hearts of himself and his companions. The second bass-relief shows Columbus reverently returning thanks to Heaven for his success. On the beach two sailors are hauling up his boat. Pressing about him, caressing his hands and kissing the hem of his robe, are grouped his companions, shedding tears of joy and entreating his forgiveness, while peeping through a screen of tropical foliage, the wondering and half frightened Indians gaze at the strangers.

The spaces between the bass-reliefs and at the sides of the Genius and the Eagle bear the following inscriptions in English and Italian, composed by Ugo Flores, the Sicilian poet :-

The English inscription reads as follows, on the sides of the base between the massive posts which form the corners :-

"TO CHRISTOPHER COLUMBUS,

THE ITALIAN RESIDENTS IN AMERICA.

SCOFFED AT BEFORE; DURING THE VOYAGE MENACED; AFTER IT CHAINED; AS GENEROUS AS OPPRESSED, TO THE WORLD HE GAVE A WORLD.

JOY AND GLORY NEVER UTTERED A MORE THRILLING CALL THAN THAT WHICH RESOUNDED FROM THE CONQUERED OCEAN IN SIGHT OF THE FIRST AMERICAN ISLAND. LAND! LAND!

———

ON THE XVIITH OF OCTOBER MDCCCXCII THE FOURTH CENTENARY OF THE DISCOVERY OF AMERICA IN IMPERISHABLE REMEMBRANCE."

The Italian inscription is :-"A CRISTOFORO COLOMBO-GLI ITALIANI RESIDENTI IN AMERICA-IRRISO PRIMA-MINACCIATO DURANTE IL VIAGGIO-INCATENATO DOPO-SAPENDO ESSERE GENEROSO QUANTO OPPRESSO-DONAVA UN MONDO AL MONDO-LA GIOIA E LA GLORIA-NON EBBERO MAI PIU' SOLENNE GRIDO DI QUELLO CHE RISUONO'-SULL' OCEANO DOMATO-IN VISTA DELLA PRIMA ISOLA AMERICANA: TERRA! TERRA!-NEL XII OTTOBRE MDCCCXCII IV CENTENARIO-DELLA SCOPERTA D'AMERICA A IMPERITURA MEMORIA."

COLUMBUS FOUNTAIN, NEW YORK CITY. - The projected Columbus Fountain for Central Park, New York, is the work of the celebrated Spanish sculptor, Fernando Miranda. The fountain is to have a basin one hundred feet in diameter. From the centre rises a section of the globe on the summit of which stands the Admiral with his two Captains, Martin Alonzo Pinzon, and his brother, Vicente Yañez Pinzon. The total height of the globe and figures above the water is to be twenty-nine feet, and the figures will be of bronze and sixteen feet high. The fountain will also be of bronze, while the proposed

70—COLUMBUS FOUNTAIN, NEW YORK CITY.

site is the Plaza at the entrance to Central Park. The artist has put the finishing touches to his model and nothing now remains to be done but the casting of the group.

The figure of Columbus is to face Fifth Avenue. The technical difficulties which the sculptor had to surmount were many. The grouping of the figures in juxtaposition was a serious problem without making a plexus of the legs, but, as will be seen from the illustrations, Mr. Miranda has cleverly overcome the difficulty. The figures stand in natural positions—Columbus grasping the cross-hilt of his sword and looking eagerly ahead, while Vicente Pinzon points with the impulsiveness of youth to the land which is dimly discernible in the distance, and Martin Pinzon shading his eyes with his left hand, is looking in the same direction as his companions. (Cuts Nos. 69 and 70.)

The dress and arms are absolutely correct, even to the lesser details of the decorations of the skirt of the tunic.

The fountain is a gift from the citizens of the Spanish race of America to the city of New York, and the Spanish government has offered to supply from her arsenals any deficiencies in metal ; a special act for that purpose having been passed by the Cortes. Several of the South American Republics have already sent their old cannon to New York, and church bells are also promised to be used in combination with the gun metal. The total weight of metal required will be 20,000 pounds.

Mr. Juan N. Navarro, the Mexican consul, and Mr. Arturo Baldasano y Topete, the Spanish consul, have rendered valuable aid in pushing the project, while the Spanish ambassador at Washington, Don Enrique Dupúy de Lôme, has so interested the Queen that she as well as the Infanta have promised to send specimens of needlework and painting, the work of their own hands—the King's present consisting of toys; all of which are to be disposed of at a fair to be held in New York.

Mr. Miranda gives the labor of years as his contribution. He is a native of Valencia, Spain, and was a pupil of the sculptor Piquer of the court of Queen Isabella II. During the Centennial Exposition he came to the United States, and has since done considerable work for leading American publications. He is the designer of a bust of Cervantes which it is proposed to place in Central Park. King Alfonso XII created him a Comendador of the Royal Order of Isabella, and he was knighted several years ago.

This fountain, which is the gift of the Spanish colony in New York, will bear an inscription which reads as follows :

"A COLON Y LOS PINZONES LOS ESPAÑOLES E HISPANO-AME-RICANOS DE NUEVA YORK."

"TO COLUMBUS AND THE PINZONS, THE SPANIARDS AND SPANISH-AMERICANS OF NEW YORK."

NEW YORK HISTORICAL SOCIETY.—The bust in the possession of the New York Historical Society, has some artistic merit, but as it is simply a duplicate of that in the Museo Capitolino, at Rome, which is entirely imaginary, it has no historical value.

SPÑOL.—STATUE OF COLUMBUS.—A replica of his famous work now in Madrid, and which is to be erected by the New York Genealogical and Biographical Society in April of this year, is now ready for dedication, the necessary funds for the purpose having been raised. Dr. Chauncey M. Depew will deliver the oration and Edmund Clarence Stedman will read an original poem written for the occasion.

As a complete description and engravings of the original monument and the statue at Madrid, is given elsewhere, it is unnecessary for me to enter into any further particulars regarding the New York replica.

STATUE AT CENTRAL PARK, NEW YORK.—Mrs. Marshall O. Roberts has presented the statue of the Admiral, the work of Miss Emma Stebbins, which stands in Central Park. The statue is seven feet high, and represents Columbus as a sailor with a mantle thrown over the shoulder. The artist has followed the facial characteristics of the Jovian type.

COLUMBUS MEMORIAL ARCH IN NEW YORK.—A competition was opened on September 1, 1892, and a prize offered for the most acceptable design for the erection of a memorial arch at the entrance to Central Park, at Fifty-ninth Street and Fifth Avenue.

The committee appointed were Richard M. Hunt, John Lafarge, Augustus St. Gaudens, L. P. di Cesnola and Robert J. Hoguet. These gentlemen awarded the prize to a design signed "Columbia" which was submitted by Henry B. Hertz, of this city. A gold medal was given to the artist, and a permanent monument of metal and bronze to the Genius of Discovery, costing $350,000, will be erected, a large part of the amount necessary for the purpose having already been pledged.

The main body of the arch is of white marble and with its fountains, its polished monolithic columns of pigeon-blood marble, its mosaic and gold inlaying, and the bass-relief work and surmounting group of bronze, will be an architectural monument of which the city may well be proud.

From the ground to the top of the bronze caravel in the centre of the allegorical group with which the arch will be surmounted the height will be 160 feet, and the entire width of the arch will be 120 feet. The opening from the ground to the keystone will be eighty feet high and forty feet wide. On the front of each pier will be two columns of pigeon-blood marble. Between each pair of columns and at the base of each pier will be large marble fountains, the water playing about figures representing Victory and Immortality. The surface of the piers between the columns will be richly decorated in bass-relief, with gold and mosaic. Above each fountain will be a panel, one representing Columbus at the Court of Spain, and the other the great Discoverer, at the Convent of La Rábida, just before his departure on the voyage which resulted in the discovery of America. In the spaces on either side of the crown of the arch will be colossal reclining figures of Victory in bass-relief.

The highly decorated frieze will be of polished red marble, and surmounting the projecting keystone of the arch will be a bronze representation of an American eagle. On the central panel of the attic will be the inscription :

"THE UNITED STATES OF AMERICA IN MEMORIAL GLORIOUS TO CHRISTOPHER COLUMBUS, DISCOVERER OF AMERICA."

The ornamentation of the attic consists of Columbus' entry into Barcelona. Crowning all. is to be a group in bronze symbolical of Discovery. In this group there will be twelve figures of heroic size, and a colossal statue representing the Genius of Discovery, heralding to the world the achievements of her children.

The designer is only twenty-one years old and is a student in the architectural department of Columbia College.

THE STATUE AT FAIRMOUNT PARK,—PHILADELPHIA.—In regard to this statue which I saw at the World's Fair in 1876, I will avail myself of a splendid work entitled *The Masterpieces of the International Exhibition of 1876*, Gebbie & Barrie, publishers, Philadelphia, from which I have taken the following data :—

" The history of this memorial is closely connected with that of the Exhibition. The Italian residents of Philadelphia, the year before the Centennial. inaugurated a movement, having for its purpose the erection of a fitting monument in memory of the Discoverer, and which should stand in the immediate vicinity of the Exhibition Building. The necessary funds were quickly raised and the first statue of Columbus ever erected in the United States by private subscription, was ordered from Italy. In 1876, Mr. Viti, the Italian Consul at Philadelphia, who was in charge of the project, received photographs of the model, and the statue was completed and dedicated before the close of the Exhibition.

" It now ornaments the beautiful grounds of Fairmount Park, near the site of the Exhibition. The monument is lofty and the figure of Columbus is of colossal proportions :—the whole structure being of the finest white marble. The statue represents the Admiral, as Discoverer, Geographer and Navigator. The position is a standing one, with the right hand resting on a globe while the fingers are on the spot representing the American Continent. At his feet, is an anchor, typifying "Navigation," while his name, CHRISTOPHER COLUMBUS, is carved in large letters on the socle beneath the figure. (Cut No. 71.)

71—THE STATUE AT FAIRMOUNT PARK, PHILADELPHIA.

"On the pedestal below, is a bass-relief representing the Admiral leaving the Pinta to plant the Castilian flag upon the beach."

MONUMENT AT SCRANTON, PA.—The Italian residents of Scranton, Pa., and vicinity, desiring to immortalize the memory of their illustrious countryman,

have erected a monument to Columbus which is the work of the distinguished
Italian sculptor, Alberto Cottini.   The statue, which is of heroic size, represents
the Admiral standing on a square marble plinth which rests on a base of the
same material.   He is attired in the garb of the Admiral of the Indies.   The
inscription on the front of the plinth reads as follows : -

1492-1892 COLUMBUS.

The design of the artist is the familiar one representing the Genoese with a
chart in his right hand and pointing exultantly to the newly discovered land
with the left.

THE WASHINGTON STATUE.—Carderera says :-" In one of the façades of
the Capitol of Washington, a beautiful group in marble representing Columbus with a symbolical female figure by his side, was erected in 1844.   This
excellent work executed at Naples, by the sculptor Persico, has glaring incon-
gruities in dress, notwithstanding the fact that the famous Discoverer is represented as being clad in a suit of armor which it is said is still in the possession
of his descendants in Italy.   Judging from the engraving before us, it will be
seen that neither the armor, nor a single detail of the dress in which Columbus
is attired, belonged to his time, but to a period of one hundred years after
wards."

I regret to dissent from the opinion of so eminent an authority as Carderera, but he never saw the statue, while I have unfortunately had the opportunity of seeing it many times.   Besides the inaccuracies that Carderera
mentions, the visage of Columbus bears no resemblance at all to the descriptions we have of him, while the attitude of the Admiral with the globe in his
hand strikes me as being supremely ridiculous ; he looks like a warrior of
the XVIIth century, playing baseball with a preposterously large ball ; his
position is also unnatural, while I cannot find words to express my surprise at
the inartistic handling of the figure of the Indian maiden.

The cost of the group was $24,000 and the sculptor was at work on it for
five years.   I do not consider it worth reproduction.

DOOR OF THE CAPITOL AT WASHINGTON.—The main central entrance of the
Capitol at Washington, is the famous bronze door, the work of the American
sculptor, Randolph Rogers, which was cast by F. von Müller, at Munich, in
1861.   The door is 17 feet high and 9 feet wide and weighs 20,000 pounds.   It
is a folding or double door and is set in a bronze casing projecting about a
foot from the leaves.   On the casing, are four figures which are allegorical
representations of Asia, Africa, Europe and America, and on the casing between
them runs a border typifying Conquest and Navigation.   The high-reliefs on
the panels show important events in the life of Columbus, and at the sides of

them are statues of sixteen of the most prominent persons who took part in the discovery. (Cut No. 72.)

The eight large high-reliefs on the panels show: 1. Columbus before the

72—DOOR OF THE CAPITOL AT WASHINGTON.

Council of Salamanca. 2. Departure of Columbus from the Convent of La Rábida for the Spanish Court. 3. Audience of Columbus at the Court of Ferdinand and Isabella. 4. Departure of Columbus from Palos, on his first voyage of discovery. 5. First meeting of Columbus with the natives. 6. Triumphal entry of Columbus into Barcelona. 7. Columbus in chains. 8. Scene at the death-bed of Columbus.

On the semicircular transom of the door, a semicircular high-relief shows the landing of Columbus on the Island of San Salvador. On the jambs of the doors, there are sixteen small statues set in niches representing : 1. The Pope Alexander VI, (Roderigo Lenzoli). 2. Pedro Gonzalez de Mendoza, the Great Cardinal, Archbishop of Toledo. 3. Ferdinand, King of Spain. 4. Isabella, Queen of Spain. 5. Charles VIII, King of France. 6. Beatriz de Bobadilla, Marchioness of Moya, who befriended Columbus. It is said that the likeness is that of Mrs. Rogers, the wife of the sculptor. 7 John II, King of Portugal, who rejected the plans of Columbus. 8. Henry VII, King of England, appealed to by Bartholomew Columbus, on behalf of his brother. 9. Fray Juan Perez, Prior of the Convent of La Rábida. 10. Martin Alonzo Pinzon, commander of the Pinta. 11. Hernando Cortes, conqueror of Mexico. 12 Bartholomew Columbus, brother of Columbus. It is said that the likeness is that of the sculptor. 13. Alonzo de Ojeda, a companion of Columbus. 14. Vasco Nuñez de Balboa, discoverer of the Pacific Ocean. 15. Amerigo Vespucci, after whom by a freak of fortune the New World was named. 16. Francisco Pizarro, conqueror of Peru.

Over the transom, is a grand head of Columbus, beneath which is an American eagle with extended wings. Between the panels and at top and bottom of the leaves of the door, are ten projecting heads. Those between the panels are historians who have written about the voyages of Columbus from his own time down to the present day, ending with Irving and Prescott. The two heads at the tops of the leaves are female heads, and the two next the floor have Indian characteristics.

In the Rotunda of the Capitol, there are four high-reliefs over the doors, one representing Columbus and the others, Raleigh, Cabot and La Salle.

THE CHICAGO FOUNTAIN.—On the site between the City Hall and the Court House building in Chicago, on the Washington Street frontage, stands a statue of Columbus, the gift of John B. Drake, proprietor of the Grand Pacific Hotel. The style of the monument is Gothic, and the base is of granite from Baveno, Italy. On the front of the pedestal will be placed a bronze statue of the Admiral seven feet high, cast in Rome; the statue is the work of Mr. R. H. Park, of Chicago.

The foundation has a receptacle holding two tons of ice, and has ten faucets, each provided with a bronze drinking cup.

The inscription reads: "ICE WATER DRINKING FOUNTAIN PRE
SENTED TO THE CITY OF CHICAGO BY JOHN B. DRAKE, 1892."

At the feet of the statue of Columbus, who is represented as a student of
geography at the University of Pavia, is inscribed:

"CHRISTOPHER COLUMBUS, 1492—1892."

The red granite base for the fountain, came from Turin, Italy.

THE ST. LOUIS STATUE.—In the city of St. Louis, Mo., in Shaw's Garden,
is a statue of Columbus, which is the gift of Mr. Shaw to the city. The figure
of the Admiral is of gilt bronze of heroic size and stands upon a granite pedestal, which has four bronze bass-reliefs portraying the principal events in
his career. The features follow the Genoa model and the statue was cast at
Munich.

THE STATUE AT SACRAMENTO, CAL.—In the State Capitol at Sacramento,
stands a beautiful and artistic group in white marble, the work of Larkin G.
Mead of Vermont, which was presented to the State of California in 1883, by
D. O. Mills. It is of white marble and represents Columbus pleading his cause
before Queen Isabella of Spain. The Spanish sovereign is represented as
seated. At her left hand kneels the first Admiral, while a page on the right
contemplates the scene of the fabulous offer of the Queen to sacrifice her jewels
to aid in the project to discover the New World. The statue was executed
by Mr. Mead, in Florence, Italy.

MEDALS.

THE MAURA MEDAL.—The Academy of Fine Arts of San Fernando established at Madrid, opened a competition for a medal to commemorate the

Discovery of America, on its fourth Centennial. The first prize was awarded to the distinguished artist, Mr. Bartolomeo Maura. He selected for the design of his medal two of the most momentous events in the career of Columbus,—the discovery of land and the reception of the Admiral by the Kings on his return.

This happy conception was splendidly elaborated by the artist as may be seen by the annexed cuts, (Nos. 73 and 74.)

73—MAURA MEDAL, OBVERSE.

74—MAURA MEDAL REVERSE, FIRST DESIGN.

A curious story is connected with this medal: in the first design submitted, a friar was kneeling in front of Columbus as if in the act of thanking God for the success of the expedition. Many persons having with good reason objected to the presence of a friar—when as is well established to-day —no ecclesiastic accompanied the first expedition, Mr. Maura made a change in this part of the medal and substituted for the figure of the friar, one of the discontented crew. He thus showed a respect for historical truth, which has, unhappily, not been followed

in many countries and especially in the United States where every Columbian fairy tale has been deemed worthy of being chronicled, in art.

75—MAURA MEDAL REVERSE, SECOND DESIGN.

The medal is three inches
in diameter and has been cast
in gold, silver and bronze ; it
is a beautiful work of art.

THE LOPEZ MEDAL.—The
second prize was awarded to
another celebrated engraver of
medals, Mr. Francisco Asis
Lopez, the designer of the famous medal commemorating
the Centennial of Calderon.
I also give a reproduction of
of it, as it has on the obverse
a magnificent bust of Columbus, taken from the descriptions and portraits which are
considered to be the most
faithful representations of the Admiral. On the reverse, is Hope, seated in
a bark guided by Faith, in her search for the New World, which is seen in
the background, and above the bark a flying figure of Victory points to the
newly discovered land. The
medal is very beautiful, though
as it is not historical but allegorical, the Commission with
excellent judgment awarded
the prize to the Maura medal.

THE ITALIAN MEDAL.—The
Italian Government has awarded the prize for a medal commemorating the Fourth Centennial
of America, to an artist, who has
modestly desired to conceal his
name, and the medal has been
engraved by the celebrated artist, Capuccio, of Genoa.

One side of the medal represents the bust of Columbus,

76—THE LOPEZ MEDAL, OBVERSE.

almost in profile. The head is beautiful and agrees with all the descriptions
of the Admiral. It seems to have been taken from the Capriolo engraving,
and the Yañez and Rincon portraits. On the right of the bust is the New
World symbolized by an Indian, and on the left, the Old World represented
by a matron, both clasping hands under a sphere typifying the World.
Beneath the bust is a condor spreading his wings in the act of flight.

The reverse represents the American Indians looking with amazement at
the extraordinary development of their country in four centuries. America

77—THE LOPEZ MEDAL, REVERSE.

appears in the air surrounded by genii, with the attributes of Commerce,
Science and Plenty. The sun rises in the background, illuminating the
apotheosis of America ; around the medal are the coats of arms of all the
American Republics. Above the allegory is MDCCCXCII, and at the exergue
under the feet of the Indians are the figures, MCCCCXCII. The medal is
very large and exceedingly beautiful. I reproduce the obverse for the
purpose of showing a new effigy of Columbus.

78—ITALIAN MEDAL.

HISTORICAL PAINTINGS AND ENGRAVINGS.

I NOW proceed to enumerate the most important historical paintings referring to Columbus that I have been able to find. I will
simply mention the titles and names of the painters of some as I have
not met with descriptions or reproductions of many of them. Of
others, I give descriptions, and engravings of a few of the most important. I have not followed the chronological order of the pictures,
but that of the events which they portray.

In order to avoid unnecessary repetitions, and so that readers who are not
familiar with the history of Columbus, may perfectly understand the significa-
tion of some of the paintings which I am about to describe, I will preface each
series with a short historical notice of the events to which they refer.

I. Some authors state that Columbus in his youth instead of indulging in
juvenile sports with other boys, spent his leisure hours in study and meditation. He generally preferred to roam on the seashore : this is the subject
of the following picture, which is beautiful but entirely imaginary.

1. CONCONI, (MAURO.) THE YOUTH COLUMBUS. Exhibited at the Paris
Exposition of 1867, and belonging to the collection of M. Marozzi, of Pavia.

II. Very little is known about the life of the future Discoverer, before he
entered the service of the Catholic Kings. Only some dry facts obscured by
many legends and fables have come down to us. It is known that if it be true
that he left Genoa in 1470, he certainly returned there in 1472, and soon left his
country forever. He then settled at Lisbon, where he married a lady of noble
birth, Felipa Moñiz, by whom he had at least, one son, Don Diego, the second
Admiral. He made several sea voyages and went as far north as Iceland, as
far west as the Azores, and as far south as the coast of Guinea, and also during
this time, he entered into correspondence with the famous astronomer, Paolo

Toscanelli, who confirmed his idea of the possibility of going to the East by taking a westward course.

It is also said that at this period Columbus submitted his plans for carrying out his great projects to the Republics of Venice and Genoa : there is not the slightest proof for this assertion, yet a distinguished artist three centuries ago, depicted one of these apocryphal episodes. The pictures referring to this period, are :

2. PICKERSGILL, (FREDERICK R.,) COLUMBUS AT LISBON, (1875.)

3. ELMORE, (ALFRED.) COLUMBUS AT PORTO SANTO, (1878.)

4. TAVARONE, (LAZZARO.) COLUMBUS EXPLAINING HIS PLANS OF DISCOVERY TO THE DOGE OF VENICE. Painted in the XVIth century and now in a private palace at Genoa.

Like all paintings from the brush of Tavarone, the design and coloring of this picture are beautiful : the accessories are strictly historical, but Italian and not Spanish, and the head of Columbus is entirely imaginary.

III. It is not possible to accurately fix the date when Columbus arrived in Spain, but according to critical researches, it must have been about 1484. He spent some time in Andalusia trying to obtain the help of some of the grandees, and lived,--as Bernaldez who was his personal friend, says,--by peddling printed books and by drawing maps. In Seville, he called upon the Duke of Medina-Sidonia, and at the Puerto of Santa Maria, on the Duke of Medina-Celi, with whom he remained two years, and from whom he obtained letters of introduction to the Queen, and to many important personages connected with the Court. Among them was Cardinal Mendoza, who obtained for him an audience with the Queen, and subsequently he had other audiences with the Kings, but they differed in their opinions as to the feasibility of his plans. The following pictures refer to this event :

5. TAVARONE, (LAZZARO.) COLUMBUS IN THE PRESENCE OF FERDINAND AND ISABELLA. Painted in the XVIth century ; in a private palace at Genoa.

From the notices which I have read regarding this picture, it seems that it possesses great merit and is still well preserved, but I have been unable to find any description of it.

6. CRESPO.--PRESENTATION OF COLUMBUS TO THE CATHOLIC KINGS.

This picture which is one of the best of the modern Spanish School, has in it only five figures : they are Queen Isabella seated on a throne, having on her right hand the Marchioness de Moya, and on the other side, her husband, King Fernando, who is standing. In front of the throne stands Cardinal Mendoza presenting Columbus, who is poorly clad, to the Catholic Kings.

The figures of the King and Queen are copied from well-known portraits, and that of the Admiral looks very much like the one in the Naval Museum. The dresses of all, as well as the accessories, are strictly accurate.

7. BROZIK. (VACZLAV.) COLUMBUS SOLICITING AID FROM ISABELLA.

70.—BROZIK.—COLUMBUS SOLICITING AID FROM ISABELLA.

This fine painting is the work of the famous Bohemian artist Brozik, a disciple of Karl Piloty. In a large and magnificently furnished chamber of the Palace at Cordova, Columbus stands before a table at which Ferdinand and Isabella are seated. On it are a number of charts and the caskets containing the Queen's jewels. With the left hand the Genoese is pointing to a chart, while the other is raised. He is surrounded by monks, high Church dignitaries, learned men and others, who, with the Kings are listening to him attentively.

All the figures are of life size and the artistic work is beautifully executed, but the details are the fruit of the artist's imagination, including the caskets containing the famous jewels, which had no connection with this scene, and which have been introduced purely for sensational effect. (Cut No. 79.)

8. LEUTZE, (EMANUEL.) COLUMBUS BEFORE THE QUEEN. In the Düsseldorf Gallery.

9. COLLIN, (ALEXANDER.) FIRST ARRIVAL OF COLUMBUS IN SPAIN, (1857.)

10. ROTHERMEL, (PETER F.) COLUMBUS BEFORE ISABELLA, (1858.)

11. ROBERT-FLEURY, (JOSEPH N.) CHRISTOPHER COLUMBUS RECEIVED AT THE COURT OF SPAIN. (1848.)

IV. Ferdinand never looked favorably on the projects of Columbus, but Isabella, more enthusiastic and sanguine than her covetous husband, interested herself in the undertaking of the bold navigator *in the threadbare cloak* and ordered a consultation to be held shortly after, for the purpose of investigating and reporting to her on his project.

Unfortunately this conference was presided over by a man who, after the first interview with Columbus, became one of his bitterest enemies, and who always opposed the Admiral apparently without reason. He was no less a man than the favorite confessor of the Queen, and a man of great influence and integrity, Fray Hernando de Talavera, who was subsequently the first Archbishop of Granada. The meetings were held at Cordova, and on the return of the Court to that city, an unfavorable report was made to the Kings. The Queen did not act as Talavera and Ferdinand desired, and instead of discarding Columbus entirely, she gave him evasive answers, putting off a positive decision for a future day.

But Columbus did not give up his plans : in the meantime, he had made a host of influential and enthusiastic friends, who had decided to assist him in the carrying out of his great undertaking, and as the Queen really favored him, thanks to the untiring zeal of his patrons, another commission was appointed, and fortunately for him on this occasion, the president was one of his most intimate friends, Fray Diego de Deza, tutor of the heir to the crown, and the other members were the professors of the University of Salamanca, the centre of learning in Spain.

An error of the author of the *Historie* has led nearly all later writers to confound the Junta presided over by the Prior of Prado, Hernando de Talavera at Cordova, and the conferences which took place at Salamanca, in the church of the Dominican Convent, then called San Esteban. The first Junta was composed of Councillors to the Crown and some cosmographers: the second was composed of Dominican friars and the professors at the University of Salamanca. The author of the *Historie* only mentions one Junta and adds that "the persons appointed by the Prior of Prado were ignorant," a remark which he would not have made of the Faculty of Salamanca, but Ulloa's version of Fernando's book is so full of corruptions and interpolations, either by Ulloa himself or by others, that at present the work which Irving once called "the corner-stone of the history of the Discovery," carries little weight as an authority. These events are illustrated in the following series of paintings :-

12. LEUTZE, (EMANUEL.) COLUMBUS BEFORE THE COUNCIL OF SALAMANCA. This painting was in the Düsseldorf Gallery, but I do not know its present whereabouts. (1841.)

13. RÖTTING, (JULIUS.) COLUMBUS BEFORE THE COUNCIL AT SALAMANCA. (1851.) Dresden Gallery.

14. PLÜDDEMANN, (HERMANN.) COLUMBUS DISPUTING WITH THE JUNTA AT SALAMANCA.

15. BARABINO, (NICCOLO.) COLUMBUS BEFORE THE COUNCIL OF SALAMANCA. This is perhaps, the most beautiful picture ever painted, referring to the history of Columbus, but it is so large that the reductions I have ordered made of it are not satisfactory. I have therefore, only taken from it the magnificent figure of Columbus, which I have reproduced on p. 41 of this work under No. 23, and on p. 40 I have given a full description of the whole picture.

16. IZQUIERDO, (D. V.) COLUMBUS BEFORE THE DOMINICANS. This picture, which is the work of the famous Spanish artist Izquierdo, represents a scene in the Dominican Convent at Salamanca. Columbus stands in the centre of a group of monks. There are the usual accessories of the globe, charts, MSS., etc., which appear in other pictures. He stands with extended hand, addressing the monks on the feasibility of his projects. The features of his face correspond with the generally accepted type, but he is bald-headed, and this is the only picture of the famous Genoese, in which I have seen him thus represented. He also wears a full white beard and mustache. (Cut No. 80.)

17. MASÓ, (FELIPE.) COLUMBUS BEFORE THE DOMINICANS. This well-known painting is from the brush of Felipe Masó, a Catalonian artist, and was painted about thirty years ago. Columbus is standing behind a table in a room of the Dominican Convent at Salamanca. In front of him is

80—IZQUIERDO.—COLUMBUS BEFORE THE DOMINICANS.

a globe by means of which he is explaining his plans to a group of monks, who are intently listening to him with expressions on their faces of more or less incredulity. In the foreground are a sleeping page and dog, with a kettle boiling on a brazier. The features of the great Genoese are typically correct, while the dress and other details in the picture are historically accurate.

18. MERINO, (IGNACIO.) COLUMBUS BEFORE THE FACULTY OF THE UNIVERSITY OF SALAMANCA.

This is a noble picture and accurate in its smallest details. Barabino misled by the *Historie* of Fernando Colombo, made the confusion already mentioned and in his grand canvas depicted Columbus in the presence of a number of ignorant and prejudiced monks. The better informed Peruvian artist showed the future Discoverer before an assemblage of more or less prejudiced men, but possessing all the learning and science of the times. They do not laugh at him, they wonder, they doubt, and think deeply over the new theories propounded by the energetic and eloquent stranger who is trying to eradicate from their minds long cherished ideas. The faces of all of his hearers express the deepest interest. They are carefully consulting books, maps and globes and are discussing the feasibility of his plans. It is almost possible to distinguish those who espouse his theories from those who are opposed to them. The figure of Columbus in the centre has all his well-known characteristics, and is really splendid. The grouping cannot be improved and all the details of the picture are of the greatest excellence. I have read that the portraits of Cardinal Jimenez de Cisneros and Fray Diego de Deza, and other distinguished ecclesiastics of the time are found in the picture. Cardinal Jimenez de Cisneros is the only one I have been able to identify, but as I am not familiar with the portraits of the other persons, I have been unable to find them.

The engraving which I have is so large that I cannot reproduce it, as the reduction to the size of these pages is very indistinct.

V. The result of the conferences at Salamanca was very different from that of the Junta at Córdova, as after the latter Columbus became a member of the royal retinue, and received from time to time certain sums of money for his maintenance. The Queen was well disposed towards him, and endeavored to come to some agreement with him, but the pretensions of the Admiral were so unreasonable, that finally in 1492, the Queen positively rejected his proposals. Columbus then left the Court and went to Huelva with his younger son, Diego, probably with the intention of leaving the boy with a brother-in-law named Muliar, who resided there, when by chance or because he had heard of the geographical knowledge of Fray Juan Perez, the Prior of the Franciscan Convent at La Rábida, near Huelva, who had been confessor of the Queen, he stopped at the Convent, asking bread and water for his child. The Prior saw him, asked him who he was and whence he came, and Columbus explained his projects and disappointments to him at length. Struck by the appearance and conversation of the stranger, the good father offered him an asylum, and sent for some friends who resided at Palos, among them the physician Garci-Fernandez and the pilot Sebastian Rodriguez, to whom he introduced the Genoese. After long consultations, they decided to send Sebastian Rodriguez bearing a letter from Fray Juan Perez to the Queen warmly recommending the enterprise.

While waiting the return of Rodriguez with a reply from Isabella, many conferences were held at La Rábida, at which the brothers Pinzon and other mariners of Palos were present by invitation of the Prior.

The messenger returned quickly bringing with him a sum of money for Columbus, to enable him to buy a horse and appear at the Court suitably dressed. The future Admiral then returned to the camp before Granada, where the Catholic Kings were holding their Court.

Painters and poets have portrayed on canvas and immortalized in verse, this episode in the life of Columbus, but unfortunately historians, desiring to lend a poetical coloring to these events, have chronicled them in such manner that this portion of the biography of Columbus is filled with innumerable contradictions.

The paintings describing this incident in the life of the Admiral, will be found under the following numbers.

19. COLUMBUS DEMANDING BREAD AND WATER FOR HIS SON AT THE CONVENT OF LA RÁBIDA.

This event is supposed to have taken place in 1491, after the Queen had declined any further negotiations with Columbus, and the despairing and broken-hearted man had decided to pass to France or England. In the foreground are Columbus and Fray Juan Perez, engaged in earnest conversation : the former is represented with white hair and holds a chart in his hand. In the back ground, is a monk serving the boy with bread and water.

The painting is in the Convent of La Rábida and is the work of an unknown artist.

20. HURLSTONE, (F. Y.) COLUMBUS DEMANDING ALMS.

21. LEUTZE, (EMANUEL) COLUMBUS AT THE GATE OF THE MONASTERY OF LA RÁBIDA, (1844.)

22. MERCADÉ, (BENITO.) COLUMBUS BEGGING FOR BREAD AT THE GATE OF THE CONVENT OF LA RÁBIDA.

23. WILKIE, (SIR DAVID.) COLUMBUS AT LA RÁBIDA.

This painting is at present in the Halford collection. The great master received 500 guineas for his work. Of course, it has great artistic merit, but is very inaccurate in detail, both as to the features of Columbus and the costumes of the times. The painting is entirely imaginary, and has no historical value. (Cut No. 82.)

24. LÁNGSE. COLUMBUS AT LA RÁBIDA.

82—WILKIE.—COLUMBUS AND THE PRIOR.

This painting was exhibited at the Paris Exposition of 1867, and was much admired : it was bought at a high price for an English gentleman. I have not been able to obtain any further particulars regarding it.

25. PLÜDEMANN, (HERMANN.) COLUMBUS AT LA RÁBIDA, (1845.)

26. LUCY, (CHARLES.) COLUMBUS AT LA RÁBIDA, (1875.)

27. GUTEPROCK, (LEOPOLD.) COLUMBUS AT LA RÁBIDA.

28. DEHODENCQ, (E. A.) COLUMBUS AT THE CONVENT OF LA RÁBIDA, (1864.)

29. MASÓ, (FELIPE.) COLUMBUS AT LA RÁBIDA, (1884.)

30. COLUMBUS EXPLAINING HIS PLANS TO THE MONKS AT LA RÁBIDA.

In this picture Columbus is represented in a room at La Rábida explaining his plans to Fray Juan Perez and the two Pinzons. He stands at a table holding a globe to which he is pointing. Behind him his son is listening and in the background are two monks standing on a balcony probably discussing the matter. The painter of this picture is also unknown, but it is like the first in the Convent of La Rábida.

31. MERINO, (IGNACIO.) COLUMBUS AT LA RÁBIDA.

This beautiful painting was exhibited at the Paris Exposition, in 1855, and was greatly admired. I am told that it is now in a private gallery in the United States, but I have not been able to ascertain the name of the owner.

32. CANO, (ALONSO.) COLUMBUS AT LA RÁBIDA.

This is another purely imaginary portrayal of the famous scene at the Convent of La Rábida, when Columbus explained his project to the monks. He is represented with white hair and beard, while the monks wear full beards and the laymen beards of different styles. The picture is worthy of the artist and one of the best of the modern Spanish Historical School. (Cut No. 83.)

VI. On his return to Court Columbus was heartily welcomed and negotiations were far advanced when his extravagant pretensions again prevented an agreement being made. He left the camp and went to Cordova with the intention of taking his other son and departing for France or England. But the efforts of his friends at last prevailed with the Queen and she sent a messenger after Columbus, who overtook him at Puente de Pinos, a long distance from the camp, and with the assurance that his conditions were accepted, he returned to Santa Fé. This event is graphically portrayed in the following painting.

33. HEATON, (A. G.) RECALL OF COLUMBUS.

This picture is in the Capitol at Washington, and has been reproduced in the new issue of Columbian stamps. It is a beautiful, but entirely imaginary work.

VII. The agreement was signed, Columbus obtaining all the honors, dignities and interest for which he had asked. The funds of the Spanish Treasury had been entirely exhausted by the protracted wars which resulted in the expulsion of the Moors, and Luis de Santángel, the treasurer of Aragon, offered to advance the sum required to the Queen. There is no painting commemorating this event, but in the great monument at Barcelona, his statue and the inscription do him ample justice. By a perversion of this fact an anecdote was invented many years afterwards which relates that the Queen offered to pawn her jewels in order to raise the money required for the enterprise, but the eminent American critic Harrisse, has proven that such an offer was never made, the Queen's jewels being already in the hands of the money-lenders, and Mendez Duro, a very distinguished Spanish naval officer and the greatest apologist of Isabella, has published a pamphlet showing that the whole story is false. Nothwithstanding this, there is a beautiful painting representing this apocryphal event by an eminent Spanish artist and the United States government has made a great mistake in perpetuating a proven

83—CANO.—COLUMBUS AT LA RÁBIDA.

falsehood by the issue of a one dollar stamp commemorating the alleged incident; thus showing on the part of the officials who ordered the said issue, either ignorance or far more love for art than for historical truth.

34. Muñoz Degrain, (Antonio. Isabella Offering her Jewels in Aid of the Enterprise of Columbus.

This picture is a really beautiful one and is strictly accurate in the minutest details. It is, however, much to be regretted that so much talent has been squandered in the depiction of an event which never took place, thus helping to falsify history.

VIII. Columbus having obtained what he desired, then started for Palos, with authority to impress two caravels and the crews for the enterprise. The following picture depicts the issuing of the edict calling for men for the expedition.

35. Publication of the Royal Edict at Palos, Relative to the Armament of the Caravels.

This painting is also in the Convent of La Rábida, and appears to be by the same hand as the two preceding ones. The scene is laid in the church of the Convent. In the foreground, his face radiant with joy stands Columbus amid a group of his friends and patrons. In the pulpit, the messenger from the Catholic Kings is reading the edict for the armament of the caravels and the impressment of the crews.

IX. The Kings had agreed to place two-thirds of the sum required to defray the expenses of the undertaking at the disposal of Columbus, and he was to raise the other third. Fortunately for him, his guardian angel, the good Prior of La Rábida, had paved his way by introducing him to the brothers Pinzon, three rich and influential shipowners and navigators of Palos. They entered energetically into the plans of Columbus, looking upon it as a very risky but profitable commercial venture, and they obtained the vessels, the men and the money required, upon conditions which have not been handed down to posterity. The expedition was fitted out by them in the best style of the time, and with vessels well adapted to their purpose. On the 3rd day of August, 1492, they sailed from the port of Palos, after having duly confessed and partaken of the Holy Communion, and bidden a sad farewell to their families. The parting was more touching as many of the members of the expedition had been impressed, and also because they sailed on a Friday and did not expect to return home safely, as it is considered a day of bad omen by sailors. This departure from Palos has been a source of inspiration for many eminent artists as will be seen by the following paintings :

36. Segni. Departure of Columbus, Peloso Gallery, Genoa.

This old picture is mentioned in a guide book of the city of Genoa, but without any description or notice whatever.

84—BALAGA—COLUMBUS BIDDING FAREWELL TO THE PRIOR.

37. BALACA. (RICARDO.) COLUMBUS TAKING LEAVE OF THE PRIOR.

This graphic representation of Columbus bidding farewell to his friend, Fray Juan Perez, at Palos, is full of life and pathos. In the immediate foreground, is a group of the relatives of the crews and their friends. There is a weeping wife and a little boy taking leave of the husband and father, while directly behind this group is the central figure, Columbus, clasping the hand of Fray Juan Perez. His boat is at the wharf, waiting to convey him to the Santa Maria, which with the other caravels, is in the background with their sails set in readiness to depart on their eventful expedition. The painting is the work of the Spanish artist, R. Balaca, and was painted by order of the late Duke of Montpensier, who married a sister of Isabella, ex-Queen of Spain. The composition and grouping are admirable. (Cut No. 84.)

38. THE EMBARKATION AT PALOS.

In the foreground, stands Columbus in his boat, taking farewell of his stanch friend, Fray Juan Perez. In the background, are the caravels, the shore, and a number of friends of the departing adventurers and the Convent of La Rábida.

This painting appears to be from the same brush as the three others in the Convent of La Rábida, but none of them have any merit either historic or artistic.

39. MERINO. (IGNACIO.) COLUMBUS BIDDING FAREWELL TO HIS SONS.

The distinguished Peruvian artist, Merino, painted this beautiful picture which obtained a prize in the Paris Salon (1861), and was warmly commended by the Press. Unluckily, I have not been able to find any detailed description of it, but in view of the other works of Merino referring to American history, I am inclined to believe that he has been as accurate in this as in his other works.

40. GISBERT, (ANTONIO.) DEPARTURE OF COLUMBUS.

This celebrated picture of the departure of Columbus from Palos is from the brush of the eminent Spanish artist Gisbert. In the foreground, are some kneeling figures, with Fray Juan Perez blessing the expedition, while immediately in front, Columbus, who is in his boat, is kneeling, his hand laid on his breast. Directly behind him, is a group of officers, knights and soldiers, while his sailors are bending to their oars, preparing to convey him to the caravels, in the background, with their sails set. (Cut No. 85.)

41. LEUTZE, (EMANUEL.) DEPARTURE OF COLUMBUS FROM PALOS, two with some slight variations. (1853.)

42. ROTHERMEL, (PETER F.) EMBARKATION OF COLUMBUS, (1870.) Pennsylvania Academy.

85.—DEPARTURE OF COLUMBUS.

X. The expedition started for the Canaries on the 3rd day of August, 1492. After touching at these Islands on the 6th of September, they steered a direct westerly course. I think it proper to introduce here the two allegorical engravings published by the famous artist, De Bry, and two paintings referring to the voyage.

43. DE BRY, (THEODORE.) THE DE BRY ALLEGORY. COLUMBUS AT SEA.

This quaint engraving shows the Admiral standing in the bow of his ship, which is near the shore. He is clad in a long mantle and undercoat, while his armor lies at his feet, and his standard is floating from the foremast. Behind him is Minerva, carrying a spear and a shield with the head of Medusa in the centre, presenting a laurel branch to Columbus. Behind the goddess is Mars in full armor, standing on the back of a turtle for a chariot, and drawn by three lions. Near him, are two Sirens, whilst at the head of the vessel, are a Mermaid and a Triton acting as pilots. In the far distance, is a flock of Harpies, typifying the sinister influences with which the Genoese had to contend. In the East is the rising sun and the territory which he had just discovered. All that can be said of it is that the engraver had a fertile imagination and that the execution of the design is beautiful. (Cut No. 86.)

44. DE BRY, (THEODORE.) COLUMBUS AT SEA.

This engraving, which is also the work of De Bry, is a companion picture to the foregoing, and is very similar to it, as may be seen from a comparison of both.

In this engraving, however, Columbus appears clad in full armor as an Admiral. (Cut No. 87.)

45. COLIN, (ALEXANDER.) FIRST VOYAGE OF DISCOVERY.

In the catalogue of the Paris Exposition of 1855, this picture is mentioned but without any further particulars.

46. MASÓ, (FELIPE.) COLUMBUS AT SEA, (1884.)

This picture was sold to one of the South American Republics, but to which one I am unable to say.

XI. At length in the early dawn of October 12th, 1492, land was sighted. I have found the following paintings of this momentous event.

47. PILOTY, (KARL VON.) THE DISCOVERY OF AMERICA BY COLUMBUS. (1865.)

This painting which, notwithstanding its theatrical and sensational character, possesses remarkable merit, is in the possession of Count von Schaack, at Munich.

It has the vigorous coloring and perfect design, so characteristic of the

86—DE BRY ALLEGORY.

eminent artist. It is to be regretted that so prominent a painter as Piloty should not have taken the trouble to render his painting historically accurate. All the figures, dresses and accessories, though admirable from an artistic point of view, are entirely imaginary. It was painted in 1866.

48. POWELL, (WILLIAM H.) COLUMBUS IN SIGHT OF LAND.

I have never seen anything but a very small and indifferent cut of this picture, but I take it for granted that it may possess some merit, since it has been reproduced in the series of Columbian stamps issued by the government of the United States.

49. JOLLIVET, (PIERRE JULES.) CHRISTOPHER COLUMBUS DISCOVERING AMERICA, (1833.)

50. ESPALTER Y RULL, (JOAQUIN.) DISCOVERY OF AMERICA, (1877.)

51. RUBEN, (CHRISTIAN.) COLUMBUS DISCOVERING LAND, (1843.) Prague Gallery.

52. PLÜDEMANN, (HERMANN.) COLUMBUS DISCOVERING LAND, (1836.) National Gallery, Berlin. Columbus leaning against a mast, raising his eyes to heaven, while the officers and crew prostrate themselves before him, and the sailors greet the land with passionate gestures.

XII. On the morning of the 12th of October, 1492, the navigators landed on an island which Columbus named San Salvador, and which was called by the natives Guanahani. The determination of the exact location of this island has caused the expenditure of much money, brains and labor on the part of investigators. The number of books, pamphlets, reviews, articles, etc., on this subject is astonishing. I believe that the very first critical historian who undertook to fix its exact position on the map, the eminent author of the *Historia del Nuevo Mundo*, Juan Bautista Muñoz, determined it accurately, declaring that Guanahani was Watling's Island. Further researches by well-known authors, especially those of Captain Becher and Rudolph Cronau, seem to confirm this assertion conclusively. The latter has explained all the discrepancies in the log-book of Columbus, by showing that the Admiral landed on the western coast of the island, having been carried by the currents beyond its northern side, where he probably saw the light to which he refers, shortly before midnight on October 11th, 1492.

Many paintings have been made representing the first landing, and I will describe those which are known to me.

53. SOLIMENE, (FRANCESCO.) THE LANDING OF COLUMBUS ON AMERICAN SOIL.

The famous Neapolitan artist Solimene, painted this work at the beginning

87—DE BRY ALLEGORY.

of the last century in the palace of the Doge. It was unfortunately destroyed in a fire in 1779. The sketches had been preserved, and Carlo Giuseppe Ratti, a disciple of Mengs, was chosen at the suggestion of his master to reproduce it, which he did in the most perfect manner, even reproducing the anachronisms in the original Solimene. It is a semicircular picture, in which Columbus is represented in the act of planting the Standard of the Cross, and taking possession of the land in the name of the Kings of Spain. The figure of Faith encompassed by clouds and surrounded by angels, stands at the head of the picture, and at the sides are graceful groups of figures which, though they may charm the eye of the artist, would not be appreciated by the historian, as not only the scenery, but the figures, costumes, animals and all the accessories are entirely imaginary.

54. CARLONE, (GIAMBATTISTA.) COLUMBUS PLANTING THE CROSS ON THE FIRST LAND DISCOVERED.

Fresco painted in 1665 in the chapel of the Ducal Palace at Genoa.

The design is excellent : Columbus is in the foreground sustaining a large wooden cross, while his followers are planting it firmly by means of wedges driven into the ground. On the left of the background, are the caravels, depicted as Genoese vessels of the XVIIth century. On the right, are *stone altars*, human remains, tents and soldiers. The types and attire of Columbus and his soldiers are fairly accurate, and the powerful head of the Admiral is beautiful and has a grand expression. According to my information this fresco is still in good preservation and its colors are fairly fresh.

55. VANDERLYN, (JOHN.) THE LANDING OF COLUMBUS, (1776-1852.)

The Landing of Columbus, by Vanderlyn, which has been reproduced in a great number of works especially educational, is one of the eight panels of celebrated paintings now in the Rotunda of the Capitol at Washington, where it was painted in 1842. This picture represents Columbus in the act of landing, and taking possession of the country in the name of the Catholic Kings : it seems to have been the intention of the painter to portray Columbus, Martin Alonzo Pinzon, Vicente Yañez Pinzon, Rodrigo Escovedo, Rodrigo Sanchez, Alonzo de Ojeda, and some other members of the crew, but none of the portraits is worth anything historically ; among those who are represented is a friar, and it is a well-known fact that no friar came to America with Columbus on his first voyage. The picture is tolerably good from an artistic point of view, but historically it is worthless. One of the vessels of the expedition is seen in the distance, and the foliage of the tropics is fairly well rendered, in the large trees on one of the sides of the picture. (No. 88.)

88—VANDERLYN—THE LANDING OF COLUMBUS.

56. PUEBLA, (DIÓSCORO.) LANDING OF COLUMBUS.

This painting is the work of the celebrated Spanish artist, Dióscoro Puebla, and represents the landing of Columbus on the Island of San Salvador, in the early morning of the 12th October, 1492. This picture is well worth a short description. In the foreground, and the central figure, is the kneeling form of the Admiral, who has just landed, saluting with his sword with his right hand and holding a standard in his left. To the right, standing under a banana tree, his left hand outstretched, and raising a crucifix in the right, is a friar. In the rear of these two principal figures, are the other members of the expedition, in the act of landing on the newly-discovered territory. In the background, are the sails and masts of the caravels. There is only one inaccuracy in the picture, which is the figure of the friar, as Columbus was not accompanied by any ecclesiastic on this voyage, but it is, nevertheless, the work of a master-hand. (No. 89)

57. HAMMAN, (EDOUARD L.) LANDING OF COLUMBUS.

This picture was exhibited at the Paris Exposition of 1855, but I have been unable to ascertain its present whereabouts.

58. CLOSS, (G. ADOLF.) LANDING OF COLUMBUS AT GUANAHANI.

This painting is in the Gallery at Stuttgart ; I have an engraving of it. The artistic treatment is good, but the painter unfortunately paid no attention to history or details of dress and other essential accessories.

59. BIERSTADT, (ALBERT.) LANDING OF COLUMBUS.

This picture was exhibited at the Centennial Exposition, Philadelphia, in 1876, but I know nothing further regarding it.

60. LEUTZE, (EMANUEL.) FIRST LANDING OF COLUMBUS IN AMERICA, (1863.)

61. DIETHE, (ALFRED.) LANDING OF COLUMBUS AT SAN SALVADOR.

XIII. Columbus continued his voyage discovering some of the small islands in the Bahamas, next Cuba, and then steering eastward he reached Santo Domingo. Pinzon had abandoned him with the Pinta, and on the night of December 24th, the Admiral went to bed. The helmsman had left the rudder in charge of a young sailor who fell asleep, when of a sudden, the vessel carried by the currents struck on a rock near Cape Haytien. The Admiral was soon on deck and tried to save his ship, but the panic-stricken sailors abandoned it, and in a short time it was totally wrecked. This event is portrayed in the following picture.

62. CLOSS, (G. ADOLF.) SHIPWRECK OF THE SANTA MARIA.

This picture is very effective and well-drawn. The bright, sunlit sky, the

82—PUEBLA—LANDING OF COLUMBUS.

sea, the rock, the shore, sea-fowl and vegetation of Santo Domingo, are well rendered. The Santa Maria is accurately painted, but the scene is lighted by brilliant sunshine, and it is well-known that the ship was wrecked and abandoned shortly after midnight.

XIV. It is not my intention to follow Columbus step by step. I will therefore proceed to the next important event depicted by painters, viz., his arrival at the Court of the Kings, and his reception by them at Barcelona. I will not describe his hazardous return voyage, his arrival at Palos, nor his triumphal progress through Spain. I will simply refer my readers, if they are fond of glowing descriptions, to the splendid but highly colored one given by Washington Irving in his now somewhat antiquated *Life of Columbus.* Oviedo, who was present at the reception, says briefly that "Columbus was very kindly and graciously received by the Kings."

Artists have given full scope to their imaginations in the portrayal of this event, as will be seen by the following paintings:

63. PELAGIO, (PELAGI.) THE RETURN OF COLUMBUS.

By order of the Peloso family, this celebrated artist painted the fresco which can yet be seen at the Peloso Gallery in their palace at Genoa: it is still in very good condition and has great merit as a work of art.

64. RECEPTION OF COLUMBUS AT BARCELONA.

In the palace of L'Annunziata, Genoa, which formerly belonged to the Ferrari family but which has often changed hands and is now known as the Coen, there is a hall solely dedicated to the memory of Columbus. The finest of its paintings is the reception of Columbus at Barcelona, but unfortunately I have not been able to ascertain the name of the artist. It is full of life and movement, but the costumes in general are inaccurate. The fauna and flora of the New World are, however, well portrayed by the artist, although he has not confined himself to the regions discovered by Columbus, but has depicted the whole natural kingdom from Greenland to Tierra del Fuego. As a work of art, it is much admired.

65. GANDOLFI. RECEPTION OF COLUMBUS AT BARCELONA.

Council Hall at Genoa.

This is a very dramatic but untruthful picture. In the Court of the Palace at Barcelona, a large graded platform has been erected specially for the occasion. On the left, in the background, are the Kings seated on chairs of state: in front of them, in the center, is Columbus standing before a chair in a very dramatic attitude, describing his voyage: in the extreme background, are buildings, ships and a large concourse of people, greeting Columbus by

30.—BALACA—RECEPTION OF COLUMBUS AT BARCELONA.

waving hands and handkerchiefs, (handkerchiefs were not known at that time.) Behind the Admiral and in front of him in the foreground are the courtiers and attendant ladies, and even a Moor in full costume. The grouping is excellent; pages are presenting fruits, birds and other products of the lands discovered to the Kings, but there are no Indians present. The people, dresses, ornaments, etc., are anything but Spanish, yet the picture is celebrated for its artistic merit.

66. BALACA, (RICARDO.)

This picture represents the scene at the reception of Columbus by the Catholic Kings in Barcelona, on his return from his first voyage. The Admiral is represented in front of the Sovereigns addressing them. He is richly dressed in the garb of an Admiral, the face is clean shaven, the hair white, and the features of his face correspond with the accepted descriptions of Columbus. The Kings are seated under a canopy on chairs of state, which are placed on a dais approached by three broad, low steps. At the back of the canopy, is an escutcheon bearing the arms of Castile and Aragon, while at the side of each of the Kings stands a herald in full Court dress, carrying a mace on his right shoulder. Seated at the right hand of the Queen is a youth, and near him is a group of the ladies of the Court. In the foreground are three chests, from which a kneeling attendant has taken Indian spears, bows, clubs, pottery, etc. Kneeling by the side of Columbus and regarding the scene with astonishment are the nude figures of four Indians of both sexes. Immediately behind the Admiral are a number of knights, courtiers and ecclesiastics, representing the most distinguished men at the Court of Ferdinand and Isabella, who, together with the Kings, are intently listening to the absorbing tale. All these figures have been taken from statues and pictures of the time. The chamber in which the reception is being held has stained glass windows, is hung with tapestry and is very lofty.

The picture is a magnificent one; it was painted by the famous Spanish artist, Balaca, and will forever reflect credit on his genius and skill. (No. 90.)

67. ANCKERMAN, (RICARDO.) RECEPTION OF COLUMBUS AT BARCELONA.

The Admiral appears in the center of the picture, kneeling on the steps of the throne and kissing the hand of Isabella, while Ferdinand stands by her side. She is surrounded by her ladies of honor. In the background of the picture to the right are a number of courtiers and military men. In the foreground on the right are seven Indians of both sexes, in different positions wondering at the splendor of the Court.

It is not only a beautiful painting, but it is correct in the details of types, attire, ornaments and architecture. The face of Columbus is very similar to that in the Naval Museum at Madrid and the lineaments of the King and Queen are the same as in their well-known portraits. The distribution of the groups is very effective, and even the number of Indians, seven, is strictly accurate historically.

68. GREGORI, (LUIGI.) COLUMBUS PRESENTING THE NATIVES TO THE QUEEN.

This picture is at the University of Notre Dame — South Bend, Indiana.

69. GONZALEZ DE RIBERA, (ANTONIO.) COLUMBUS OFFERING A NEW WORLD TO THE CATHOLIC KINGS.

This large fresco is painted on the ceiling of Hall No. 21, in the Royal Palace at Madrid. I have examined guide-books of Madrid, and have questioned many of my friends who have resided there, in regard to this picture, but to my great regret I have not been able to obtain any more information about it than the simple notice found in one of the guide-books. However, as the painter was a talented artist, I suppose it deserves more than a passing notice.

70. COLIN, (ALEXANDRE MARIE.) RECEPTION OF COLUMBUS BY THE CATHOLIC KINGS.

This picture apears in the Catalogue of the Paris Salon of 1861.

71. DEVERIA, (EUGÈNE.) RECEPTION OF COLUMBUS BY FERDINAND AND ISABELLA. (Paris Salon, 1861.)

72. PLUDDEMANN, (HERMANN.) ENTRY OF COLUMBUS INTO BARCELONA. (1842.)

73. LEUTZE, (EMANUEL.) RECEPTION OF COLUMBUS ON HIS FIRST RETURN FROM AMERICA. (1847; in the Düsseldorf Gallery.)

XV. The famous engraver, Theodore de Bry, published in his *Collection of Voyages*, an apocryphal story which has been widely circulated. He avers that after Columbus returned from his first voyage, he was generously entertained by some of his friends. One of them, Cardinal Mendoza, gave a banquet in his honor and some of the grandees at the table murmured at Columbus occupying the place of honor, as he was not a man of noble birth, and went so far as to declare that any man present would have discovered the Indies just as Columbus had done. The Admiral took an egg and asked if any of the guests could stand it upright on the table. All tried to do it but without success. Then Columbus slightly broke the top of the egg and stood it on the table, observing that he had discovered the Indies just as he had found a way of standing the egg on end. This anecdote, which was first related by de Bry, was the origin of the following engraving and paintings.

74. DE BRY, (THEODORE.) COLUMBUS AND THE EGG.

I reproduce this engraving, No. 91, from the seventh plate of the fourth part of the *Voyages of De Bry*, (Frankfort, 1594.)

91—COLUMBUS AND THE EGG.

75. HOGARTH, (WILLIAM.) COLUMBUS AND THE EGG.

This picture represents a man with a full beard, holding an egg in his hand and in the act of making some explanation. The features are of the Montanus type, but the painting is entirely imaginary. Notwithstanding the usual accuracy of Hogarth in all his works, in this instance he did not pay the slightest attention to the descriptions of Columbus that have been handed down to posterity by his contemporaries. It has great artistic merit, but historically, it is absolutely worthless, as all the figures portrayed in it are of the most common-place and burlesque type.

XVI. The saddest and most dramatic episode is his imprisonment and return to Spain in chains by order of the brutal Bobadilla. This was on his return from the third voyage. As a criminal, heavily ironed, he crossed for the sixth time, that Sea of Darkness which his genius had opened to his contemporaries. Poets and painters have vied with each other in depicting this sad event. I will describe the most important pictures relating to it.

76. DUVAL, (CHARLES.) IMPRISONMENT OF COLUMBUS. (Paris Salon, 1861.)

77. MENOCAL, (ARMANDO.) THE FALL OF COLUMBUS.

I have only a very indifferent photograph of this painting. Aside from some short notices in the Havana papers, I have read three articles regarding it. One is from the pen of one of the most gifted sons of Cuba, the eloquent orator and eminent writer, Manuel Sanguily: another by the accomplished art critic of Havana, Aniceto Valdivia, widely known under his *nom de plume*, "Conde Kostia," and the last by an anonymous but very able writer on the staff of the *Union Constitucional*, a journal published in Havana. From these articles I will endeavor to give a short description of the picture, and the writers' opinions regarding it. I must add that it will be exhibited at the Chicago World's Fair.

I will commence by stating that Menocal, although still a very young artist, has attained a prominent rank in his profession, as he follows the established traditions of the old Spanish School and is a hard worker.

The picture represents Columbus in the act of stepping into the boat, ready to take him to the ship in which he is to sail for Spain, as a prisoner, by order of his brutal foe, Bobadilla. He is fettered, and Captain Vallejo, in armor, holds his hand, aiding him to enter the boat, in which there are already three sailors and two guards: behind the Admiral, are his two brothers, also fettered and surrounded by a strong guard. In the center of the foreground, is a priest with folded hands, looking sadly at the pathetic scene. Other passengers are taking leave of their friends, and some of the onlookers seem to deplore the disgraceful proceeding. On the sea in the background the vessel is lying at anchor which is to carry the Admiral. On the other side is a tropical landscape. The grouping is excellent and all the accessories are strictly historical.

According to the above-mentioned critics, the coloring is superb, and the sea, the sky and the land are as beautiful as can be depicted by the painter's brush.

Sanguily says: "The light is astonishing and wonderful..... it seems impossible to achieve such a marvel with the brush..... it must be seen..... It is necessary to stand before that colossal canvas in order to understand the deep pathos resulting from the happy conception of the artist, the dazzling and wonderful richness of coloring of the Cuban painter. Perhaps some may find fault with the picture—that may mean that it is not perfect—Granted—but place yourself before it in a proper position, and then deny, if you can, that you are looking at something perfect."

Valdivia says: "Every one who has seen it has been surprised at the marvelous coloring and the wonderful execution of the painting. It is impossible to crown misfortune with more greatness..... all the figures on shore are in motion..... the portion of the picture showing the bark is of the first order... the sea breaking against the reefs..... the foam raised by the restless sea..... the moving horizon form a really wonderful painting."

The anonymous writer says: "At a glance, it shows that Menocal is a master in painting the human form. The Christopher Columbus that he has painted, tall, thin, old, bent by misfortunes, is the ideal type of the Discoverer of America..... Menocal studied at Madrid the works of the great masters, and has returned to Havana possessing an original style, and versed in all the secrets and resources of the Spanish School, which he knows how to skilfully employ. This picture is admirable in color and design, in relief and in the life of its subjects. Menocal is destined to be a glory to Spain and to Cuba.'

I take pleasure in acknowledging that I am indebted for these notices and a photograph of the picture, as well as for almost all the details and reproductions of monuments and paintings in Cuba, to the kindness of a prominent Cuban lawyer, Mr. Carlos I. Párraga, of Havana.

78. PLÜDDEMANN, (HERMANN). COLUMBUS IN CHAINS LANDING AT CADIZ.

79. JOVER, (FRANCISCO.) COLUMBUS RETURNING IN CHAINS.

This interesting and finely executed painting portrays one of the most pathetic incidents in the life of the Admiral—his return to old Spain in chains—after the third voyage. He is represented as wearing fetters on the left wrist and with both legs manacled and chained. He is seated at a table on which are writing materials which he has evidently just been using. On his right hand stand the Captain of the vessel and another officer, pleading with him to allow the removal of the chains. With his right hand he is

92—JOVER—COLUMBUS RETURNING IN CHAINS.

waving them away, and refusing to listen to their well-meant solicitations. He wears a fur-trimmed robe with a coat beneath it extending to the knees, and confined at the waist by a girdle. His hair is snow-white, and the dejected expression and attitude are those of one who has lost all hope and is plunged in deep despair: (No. 92.)

80. MURATON, (ALPHONSE.) COLUMBUS IN CHAINS.

My friend, the distinguished artist, Mr. Juan Peoli, has shown me the valuable original sketch of this picture, which was presented to him by the artist. It represents Columbus in chains on board of a ship, and in the background are seen some Indians, who are being sent to Spain as prisoners. Columbus is standing; he wears a scarlet coat and a cap of the same color; the features and the dress are strictly historical.

I saw the finished picture in this city some years ago, but I cannot remember in what collection. I have also seen an engraving of it, but have not been able to obtain a copy.

81. PORTMAN, (CHRISTIAN J. L.) COLUMBUS IN CHAINS SENT TO EUROPE. (1840.)

82. LEUTZE, (EMANUEL.) THIRD RETURN OF COLUMBUS FROM AMERICA. (1842.) Providence, R. I.

83. WAPPERS, (GUSTAAF.) COLUMBUS IN IRONS.

This is a beautiful picture. I have reproduced the most important part, the portrait of Columbus, in cut 24, page 42, where I state my reason for not having reproduced the entire picture.

84. MARÉCHAL, (CHARLES L.) COLUMBUS BROUGHT BACK IN CHAINS.

This magnificent water-color was formerly in the collection of Prince Napoleon. Years ago I saw a beautiful engraving of it, but have never been able to find another. The description by the eminent critic Maxime du Camp, says among other things: "All the suffering that human nature can bear is imprinted upon that thoughtful face resting on the contracted hand. It is the desperation of a man of genius who apparently begins to doubt the existence of a God. There are many paintings 100 feet square which do not contain the burning pathos and the great drama shown in this water color, the most beautiful that I have ever seen. Mr. Maréchal has given a sublime reality to a popular tradition." (1851.)

XVII. The brutal conduct of Bobadilla to Columbus greatly displeased the Catholic Kings. Immediately after the arrival of the Admiral they gave orders for his release, sent him a large sum of money, and ordered him to appear at once before them. When he reached the Court he was received with

COLUMBUS BEFORE THE CATHOLIC KINGS.—BRUZZI.

the highest marks of favor, and was reinstated in all his honors and titles. At another audience he had an opportunity to give a detailed account of his third voyage. A great and well-known Spanish painter and a distinguished German painter have portrayed these events in the following paintings.

85. JOVER, (FRANCISCO.) COLUMBUS DESCRIBING HIS THIRD VOYAGE TO THE CATHOLIC KINGS.

The Admiral is represented as narrating the story of his voyages to the Kings, who are attentively listening to him. This picture, like all those on Spanish subjects of the modern Spanish school, has the great merit of accurately following the most minute details of the types, dresses, ornaments, furniture and architecture of the day. (See cut No. 93.)

In the central group are the Kings, and on their left stand the Marchioness of Moya and other ladies of the Queen's suite. On the right of Ferdinand stand Deza and a lady of the Court. On the left of the picture is the group showing the seated figure of Columbus, and three courtiers standing behind his chair.

The features of Columbus and of the Kings are admirable in expression, and the picture is of great artistic merit.

86. LEUTZE, (EMANUEL.) KING FERDINAND REMOVING THE CHAINS FROM COLUMBUS. 1843.)

87. JOVER, (FRANCISCO.) COLUMBUS REINSTATED IN HIS HONORS.

XVIII. The last days of Columbus and his death form the subject for the two pictures now to be described.

88. (JACQUAND, (CLAUDIUS.) COLUMBUS ON HIS DEATH-BED, SHOWING HIS CHAINS TO HIS SON. (1870.)

89. EDWARD, (MAY.) LAST DAYS OF CHRISTOPHER COLUMBUS, OR COLUMBUS MAKING HIS WILL. Paris Salon, 1861.

90. WAPPERS, (GUSTAAF.) DEATH OF COLUMBUS.

This is a very dramatic picture. Columbus blesses his son who is kneeling by his side. The chains are seen over a large chest. There is a beautiful engraving of it by Devachez.

91. PLÜDDEMANN, (HERMANN.) DEATH OF COLUMBUS. 1840.

92. ORTEGA, (FRANCISCO.) DEATH OF COLUMBUS.

This powerful and artistic painting represents the death-bed of Columbus, the closing scene of his eventful and unhappy life. The Admiral is lying on a miserable pallet in a meanly furnished room of a poor inn at Valladolid. The coverlid is drawn over the lower portion of the face. Around him are his friends, Diego Mendez, kneeling at the foot of the bed, and some

94—ORTERIA DEATH OF COLUMBUS.

monks, together with certain of his relatives, while his son kneels at the head of the bed with his face buried in the pillows and his arm supporting the head of his father. (No. 94.)

XIX. The following are allegorical pictures referring to Columbus and his discoveries.

93. THE TRIUMPH OF COLUMBUS, from a drawing supposed to be by himself.

This drawing has been taken from a MS. kept in the Ducal Palace at Genoa, it being supposed that the design is from an original sketch by Columbus himself. It is enclosed in a frame about 10 x 8 inches. In the center of the picture is Columbus sitting in a chariot, whose wheels are bearing him through a boisterous sea, in which are dimly seen some monsters, typifying Envy and Ignorance, his greatest enemies. Providence sits by the side of the Admiral. Two sea-horses representing Constancy and Tolerance, are drawing the chariot which is pushed by the Christian Religion, and in the air above Columbus are Victory, Hope and Fame. (No. 95.)

94. ALEU, (RAFAEL.) THE APOTHEOSIS OF COLUMBUS.

The celebrated Spanish artist Aleu, in painting this picture now at Madrid, has availed himself of a sketch which is supposed to have been drawn by Columbus, now in the City Hall at Genoa, and in which the Admiral depicts his own apotheosis. I have already described and reproduced this drawing. The painter has not closely followed the original idea.

In the foreground Europe, Asia and Africa gaze wonderingly at the scene before them, listening to the trumpet blast of an allegorical figure of Fame. In another part of the picture, and above a cloud, is a group of Red Indians contemplating Columbus with astonishment. He appears enveloped in clouds, and radiant with dignity and majesty, seated in a golden car in the shape of a shell, symbolical of the frail caravels, which is driven by a figure representing Providence. In the background are two angels placing the crown of Viceroy of the Indies on the head of the Admiral, and a throng of illustrious men is seen through the mist applauding the great deeds of the Discoverer. On the border of the picture are the portraits of Isabella, Fernando, Fray Antonio Marchena, Juan de la Cosa, Martin Alonzo Pinzon and Juan Perez. At the head of the picture is the coat of arms of Spain, at the foot is that of Columbus, while at the sides are those of eight of the most important cities where the principal events in the life of the Admiral occurred, viz: Genoa, Huelva, Granada, Salamanca, Barcelona, Seville, Cadiz and Valladolid.

95. CHENAVARD, (PAUL J.) CONQUEST OF THE NEW WORLD.

Théophile Gautier gives the following description of this magnificent com-

95—TRIUMPH OF COLUMBUS.

position which was intended for a fresco in the Pantheon. "The Admiral's vessel, commanded by Columbus, is seen standing crosswise in the foreground, which is formed by the breaking waves. In the high castle on the poop, built after the singular fashion of the naval constructions of those times, Christopher Columbus stands, surrounded by his Spaniards and some Indian captives; the sailors and the slaves are loading the ship, which lies off the land, with lumps of virgin gold, strange idols, feather mattresses, birds, parrots of brilliant plumage, and all that European research was able to plunder from that world, unveiled as the Eldorado of adventurers."

There is an admirable engraving of this cartoon by Hanf Staengl.

96. HUNT, (WILLIAM MORRIS.)

In the *American Art Review* I find an article by Mr. F. P. Vinton, in which he describes a picture by the American artist, William Morris Hunt, representing the Discoverer. Columbus is in a barque, steered by Fortune and three allegorical female figures representing Hope, Science and Faith accompany him. The opinion of Mr. Vinton is not very favorable to the painting, of which I have seen only a very indifferent engraving. The picture is in the new Capitol at Albany.

97. HAMILTON, (JAMES.) VISION OF COLUMBUS.

In the possession of Mrs. Joseph Harrison, Philadelphia, Pa.

XX. The celebration of the first mass on the New Continent and in the city of Havana, are commemorated in the following pictures.

98. THE FIRST MASS IN AMERICA.

This splendid work is from the brush of a young Cuban artist, José Arburu y Morell, who was born at Havana, in 1864, and died in Paris, in 1889, before he was 25 years of age. He first studied at the Academy of San Alejandro, Havana, under Melero, and afterwards at the Academy of San Fernando, Madrid, under the direction of Dominguez. He was also a distinguished sculptor, and was awarded the first prize for his painting, "The First Mass in America," in a competition opened in 1888 by *La Ilustracion Española y Americana*, of Madrid. The picture was warmly commended by such eminent artists as Pradilla and Plasencia, and in the opinion of painters should have been on a canvas of 20x25 feet in length, but the painter had not the necessary funds for such a large work.

I am indebted for these notes and a description of this splendid picture, written by Julian Casal, to the kindness of my friend, Mr. José Ramirez de Arellano, of Havana, who also sent me a photograph and an engraving, from which it is impossible to take a satisfactory copy:

"Under a light-blue sky dotted with rose, amber and violet-colored clouds, is seen the calm, blue surface of the ocean, flecked with snowy foam. The dim gray line of the horizon is merged in the vastness of the sea. On the shore, to the left of the spectators, a large canopy has been raised, and the wind is rustling the folds of the canvas, under which, on a crimson carpet, and against a gigantic tree, stands an altar. A priest with a long beard, robed in a white cassock fringed with gold, and attended by a fair-haired acolyte, celebrates mass, and is represented in the act of blessing his congregation, the members of which are grouped on the right, some standing and some kneeling. In front of them and closer to the altar, saluting with his sword, and holding a standard in his left hand is the venerable figure of the Admiral, his gray hair shining under the rays of the sun. That austere face furrowed by grief and misfortune, beams with benevolence and modesty. He appears to be deaf to the cheers of one of the most enthusiastic of his followers who stands behind him, and devoting his entire attention to the religious ceremony.

Near the great Genoese is a Dominican friar with his cowl thrown back and praying fervently. The persons assembled in the background are in various positions, and the expressions on their faces are different. The grouping is splendid. On the left are a number of copper-colored Indians with bristling hair, half-naked and crouched near the altar, showing in their large black eyes, wonder or indifference. The whole composition which, but for the genius of the artist would have bordered on the theatrical, is heroic, grand and touching."

99. VERMAY, (JUAN B.) FIRST MASS IN AMERICA.

In the Templete at Havana, there is a picture representing the first mass celebrated in America, on the spot where Havana was first founded, on the southern coast of Cuba. It was said by one of the priests who accompanied Columbus on his second expedition, and it is supposed that the Admiral was present on the occasion. I last saw this picture about thirty years ago, and have entirely forgotten its details. Perhaps, it did not attract my attention on account of the bad light in which it is placed; yet as this picture and the two others in the same building are from the brush of the distinguished French painter, Juan B. Vermay, I suppose that they must possess considerable merit.

XXI. The following five pictures I cannot properly include in any particular series, for the reason that all I know about them is that I have seen them mentioned in various catalogues, but with no description. I do not even know whether they are portraits or paintings, but as they are all the works of distinguished artists, I have thought proper to at least mention them.

100. HARTE, (S. A.) COLUMBUS AND THE CHILD.

101. KEYSER, (NICAISE DE.) COLUMBUS WITH HIS SON LEAVING BARCE-
LONA.

102. MASÓ, (FELIPE.) COLUMBUS AND HIS SON. (1875.) Valparaiso
Museum.

103. COLIN, (ALEXANDER.) CHRISTOPHER COLUMBUS. (1846.)

104. HAMMAN, (ÉDOUARD JEAN.) CHRISTOPHER COLUMBUS. (1869.)

To this long list I must add that there is a very large number of pictures,
both in private and public galleries, which are entirely unknown to me, and
many others which have been destroyed by fire, shipwreck or other accidents.
I have read that about the middle of the sixteenth century, il Fiazello, other-
wise called il Sarzana, painted a number of large canvases illustrating the
history of Columbus for the Ducal Chapel at Genoa, and that they were
destroyed in a terrible conflagration in the following century. I have also
read that two pictures illustrating events in the life of Columbus, were
destroyed by the Communists at the Tuileries, in Paris, and that in the
Durazzo and Santi palaces at Genoa there are beautiful pictures referring to
Columbus; also that Scaramuzza painted by order of the Faragiano family
some splendid pictures in the Acquaverde palace, and that in the Hall of
Deputies at Madrid there are some other paintings relating to the discovery
of America. I can only mention them, as I have been unable to obtain
any further information or any descriptions of these pictures.

GENERAL INDEX.

PORTRAITS—Continued.

MONUMENTS, STATUES, ETC.

MEDALS.

HISTORICAL PAINTINGS.